The Day My Life Changed

The Day My Life Changed

Published by SILVERDALE BOOKS
An imprint of Bookmart Ltd
Registered number 2372865
Trading as Bookmart Ltd
Blaby Road
Wigston
Leicester LE18 4SE

© 2006 Magpie Books, an imprint of Constable & Robinson Ltd

Constable & Robinson Ltd
3 The Lanchesters
162 Fulham Palace Road
London W6 9ER
www.constablerobinson.com

This edition printed 2006

ISBN-10: 1-84509-420-4
ISBN-13: 978-1-84509-420-1

Font used within this book: Book Antiqua

Printed in the European Union

5 7 9 10 8 6

Contents

Introduction

Life Changing Experiences

There are a thousand different ways that people's lives can change completely from one day to the next. For some people, life is a simple progression from one moment to the next, with no great turbulence or upheaval along the way. For many others, life is a series of leaps and lurches from one crisis or moment of excitement to the next. And for others, life moves along in a way that seems predictable, predestined and simple – until something suddenly turns everything on its head, and life is never the same again.

This book is about those moments, when lives are transformed and changed by the passing effects of hard experience, by crises or by everyday realizations and revelations.

Last year I worked on a collection of accounts of people's meetings with angels. One of the aspects of that research that I found most fascinating was the way that people shared personal experiences with me that had clearly meant a great deal to them.

There were quite a few stories that people shared with me that didn't seem to fit into a book about angels. In some cases it was unclear that the experience that the teller had undergone was actually related to angels. In other cases they had simply contacted me because they wanted to share their story, even though they didn't truly feel that there was any angelic connection.

Personally I found many of these stories deeply inspiring because they revealed a depth to the human spirit that the tellers had managed to connect with in difficult, impossible or unimaginable situations. Others were inspiring for a different reason – because they revealed such a basic joy and appreciation for the simple pleasures of everyday life.

Hearing these kinds of stories is extraordinary because it reminds us of how remarkable and intriguing human beings can be. Some of the stories were disturbing, some were downright strange, but all of them taught me something about people.

As I worked on the book I started to think that it would be fascinating to collect some of these stories in a different book, one that made no assumptions about religion or spirituality, but that simply explored the ways that people's lives can be affected by their experiences.

So I once again took out advertisements in newspapers, magazines and forums asking people to send me stories about the day that changed their life. I kept this appeal deliberately simple, because part of the fascination for me was to see what kinds of stories people would volunteer, given this broad request – "to tell me about one particular day that changed their life".

I had many emails, faxes and letters from around the world in response to my advertisements. In many cases I was able to follow up on the initial contact with meetings, further correspondence or personal interviews. The stories I have included here are therefore a mixture of people's own writing, and transcripts of conversations.

Before going any further I want to thank everyone who participated in any way in the making of this book. It was a wonderful experience for me – as well as a humbling one.

It makes me feel very small to hear about the amazing

range of experiences that people have had, and I can only be grateful that so many people have taken the time to share the wealth of their experience with me.

How The Book Is Organized

It was no easy task to sort these accounts into categories. I considered having them in no particular order, and simply letting the reader dip in to different stories with no clue as to what might happen.

However it seemed to me that there were certain themes that entries had in common, and that in some cases these might strike more or less of a chord with a particular reader. I have for that reason separated the book into rough chapters, arranged by theme.

There were some themes that came up regularly in my correspondents' reports. For instance there were many correspondents who wrote to me about near-death experiences, or about the lessons they learned from times of crisis.

Other people wrote to me about tiny moments – overheard remarks, fleeting meetings with strangers or sudden realizations that had made them reassess their lives from a new perspective. In some cases these were moments from the teller's childhood, moments that guided the future course of that person's life. In other cases people told me about the lessons they only learned as they grew older, or later, as they watched their children growing up.

I felt that sorting the accounts into these categories created an interesting context for each tale. In many cases one can compare and contrast the different experiences that people have had, and can examine the variety of ways that people react to their environments.

Introduction

At the start of each chapter I have made a few comments to introduce the topic and to point out some of the themes that I think come through from the assortment of experiences assembled there. But each time I look at these stories I notice different moments and different aspects of the way that people see their lives, so the way I have sorted the chapters is by no means the perfect way of viewing the collection. You might prefer to skip my opening remarks and simply dip into the stories at random.

Be warned though that these are not all happy tales. Some are sad, some are frustrating, and some are told with bitterness or sorrow. It can be a roller coaster of emotions going from one account to the next. Certainly I found it to be that way.

However I feel that even in the worst of experiences we can see the humanity of the teller, and we can learn from how they have stood up to the sufferings they have experienced. There are also other stories here that fill me with joy or awe every time I think about them – stories of resilience, revelation and epiphany.

One other thing that I should mention is that a few people asked me not to use their real names. In these cases, where there are people who might be hurt if they identified the teller, we have used alternative names. For the same reasons, in some cases the geographical place given to identify the story is a broad identification rather than a specific town.

In general, I only asked for the most basic information about identity. I feel that people are happier to tell you their stories if they don't feel that they have to fill in a questionnaire about their lives, and the most important thing here, was to encourage people to communicate their stories. The information given is intended merely to give the reader a very broad idea of who is telling their story.

In the end, how you read this book is up to you. The accounts I have chosen for the book fascinated me for a wide variety of reasons. I didn't look for only positive inspiring stories, nor did I look only for stories that showed the worst of human nature. For me, the most fascinating thing about people is the way that they can combine the earthly with the angelic, the best with the worst.

The lives that people live are so varied, often in ways that seem arbitrary and incomprehensible regardless of whether or not we have faith in a higher being. We can't judge other people's lives without having lived them ourselves, and that of course is not possible. We can only actually live our own lives.

We do, however, have the gift of speech, and we can communicate with one another. It is possible for us to share moments and insights with each other, and my hope is that this book is something that allows us at least a momentary, fleeting insight into the souls and thoughts of the friends and strangers with whom we live every day.

Childhood's Formative Experiences

Childhood can be such an emotional assault course. Reading people's stories of childhood moments that transformed their lives is an experience that can be anything from exciting to strange to heart-rending.

The smallest details of childhood can leave marks on a young person in a way that adults never imagine. But in other cases children live through the most appallingly difficult experiences without a scar, and one little moment of joy may be what inspires them to remember their childhood in later life.

Reading these stories I was struck by the way that little children can accept these huge changes with an almost stoic calm. But these moments of upset or joy often stayed with them, and sometimes formed the way that they went on to relate to other people and to new experiences for the rest of their lives.

When one writer came to realize that his mother was fairly unstable, he felt that he reacted by becoming emotionally distanced in order to protect himself from disappointment. In another case, a young boy takes a very different lesson from the experience of losing everything in a house fire – the experience makes him less scared of change because he feels that because he had already survived huge upheaval, there is no fear in other types of change.

Who can say how children's characters are formed. The experiences narrated here may not entirely explain why someone has developed the character they have. Analysts can spend years trying to find the under-

11

lying causes of behaviour and still not succeed. It would be therefore presumptuous to assume that anyone's character is fully formed by a single incident.

But on the other hand, these are key memories in the lives of children and it is clear that they have had profound effects. Parents separating or dying, adoption, starting school or moving to new places: these are all things that would still have a major effect on our lives as adults, but when children are asked to cope with dramatic changes, the experience becomes a part of their education about the world.

And for other children here, the change is less dramatic – a change of appearance or a personal realization about one's own importance in the scheme of things can still be a big matter to a small mind. These stories are a mixture of happy and sad, positive and negative, but in every case the child has been challenged by a real change and has learned something about the world as a result.

Kenzie, 34
Scotland

I remember the day I was adopted. My mum died when I was only two, and no one knew who my dad was. There was no one to look after me so I ended up in a children's home. I don't remember anything before the children's home at all. But I remember that place well. It was a very bleak place to live. I mean they tried, and we had toys and books and everything. But every child there knew that they weren't wanted, and that's a terrible thing.

I didn't really expect anything ever to change. People did leave sometimes, although they often also came back for one reason or another. Then one day when I was six, I was introduced to a couple who were maybe going to adopt me. I was polite to them, but I didn't really understand. One afternoon they came and spent the afternoon with me, playing with toys and reading a book to me. They seemed nice enough.

A few weeks later, the warden asked me to come into his office and explained that I would be leaving the next morning to move in with this couple. He told me I had to be on my best behaviour so that they would be happy with me, and went on and on at me about what good people they were to give me a home. It all sounded more scary than exciting.

They came the next day and collected me in a big car – I remember the smell of the leather on the seats, and watching the home disappear behind me as we left. But I still believed I'd be going back so it wasn't a big emotional thing. I'd said goodbye to my friends, but no one made a

13

fuss about things like that there. No one really wanted to be emotional about anything.

When we got to the house they showed me my room, which was all prepared with an aeroplane mobile and nicely painted walls. That was exciting because I hadn't had my own room at the home.

I didn't really know what to do so I sat in there looking at a book for a while. Then it was time for some food and a bath and I went to bed. The next morning I stayed in my room again – I think I was a bit scared really. They asked if I wanted to come out and I said no.

After a while I came out, and found that the man wasn't there, but the woman was. She was called Linda. It looked like she had been crying so I asked her if she was alright and then she started crying again. She said she was worried that I didn't like being there. I told her she shouldn't get upset and how much I liked my room. I hadn't really said anything before that so you can see why she was worried. She was so relieved she gave me a big hug. I'd hardly ever been hugged but I remember liking it a lot.

After that things got better. Much better. These days I just call them my Mum and Dad, and I remember my childhood as a lovely time from then on. I'll always be grateful to them for giving me a chance.

Julia, 33
Michigan

When I was younger I was quite an awkward, ungainly child. I didn't exercise much and I ate badly and so inevitably I was overweight. I used to get teased at school and I was quite unhappy. My mother used to encourage me, by telling me that you don't need to be stick thin or perfect to be beautiful. She helped me a lot and I started to feel a bit better about myself.

One day, it would have been about ninth grade, my dad had a few of his friends around and they were sitting out in the yard having a beer. I was upstairs in my room reading, and I could hear them talking.

This guy Dave, who I never liked much, was boasting about how his kid was in the football team, and then he asked my dad how old I was. When my dad answered, Dave said "Yeah, she might even be pretty if she lost some weight. A lot of weight."

Now that was a mean thing to say, and I expected my dad to defend me. But instead, when the guys laughed, my dad just joined in with them. That was the hurtful thing – the way my dad responded. I realized that actually he was disappointed in me and didn't love me the way I thought he did.

Overhearing that changed things for me in a few different ways. First I didn't get on with my dad after that. I realized he was quite boorish and just one of the guys, like the kind of dumb boys at school who hung out in gangs. I don't think he ever knew why I started being more difficult and distant with him, but it definitely made a big difference.

15

Secondly, I became quite depressed for a few months. My mum had spent all that time building up my confidence and that one chance remark shot it to pieces again. I kind of gave up on my appearance, just wore big baggy clothes and didn't make any effort at all. My mum tried to lift me up, but while I appreciated that she was trying I just couldn't believe her when she told me things would be fine.

In the end I don't know why I came through that. I think I just suddenly realized that no one else could do it for me, so I tried to sort myself out. I started eating healthy food.

I'd tried dieting before, but hadn't done it right, and the main thing is I'd never mixed it with proper exercise. Now I started to go for a run in the morning, then walk to school (partly because I didn't want to talk to my dad in the mornings). I swam regularly, and did exercises in the early evening. And it all made a huge difference to me.

I didn't suddenly turn into a model type or anything. I'm not what you would call a natural beauty in any case, and even when I'm in good shape, I'm quite big boned. I know I'm not about to go to Hollywood. But getting fit made the biggest difference to how I felt about myself, and I think other people could see that and responded to it by respecting me a bit more.

I ended up with a real boyfriend and some good friends, and I even enjoyed those last few years of school. It turned out that my mum had been right all along – it really was about how I felt about myself, and you don't need to be pretty to feel good about yourself.

Maybe I had to go through that real low to work things out for myself. I never got on with my dad the way I once had, but I also think it's only natural for things to change when you turn from being daddy's little girl into a grown woman. I get on with him at family occasions and Christmas and everything, and I don't blame him for anything that goes wrong in my life.

But I love my mother more because I think she was always on my side when I needed her.

Tom, 40
Manhattan

My life changed completely the day my family moved to New York. I grew up in Maine, out in the woods, and I had been used to a completely rural way of life. I hadn't been to a town with a population of more than a few thousand people in it my whole life.

My dad got a new job when I was nine. He'd already been working for a New York company, but because he was a travelling salesman, covering the North East states, there was no need for him to live in the city. But after he was offered a desk job, he moved the family to the city. My mother was happy about it because she had grown up there, and I was excited because it was such a big change, even though I was also a little scared and knew I was going to miss my friends.

We moved on a bright summer day in June. We had to leave early so I was tired. I stayed awake almost all the way in the car (the furniture and everything was going in a separate van). Then I fell asleep somewhere in Connecticut and missed the ride into New York. But my dad woke me up as we got to the river. I'm not sure which

17

bridge we came over, but I remember being awestruck by the Manhattan skyline. It's such a beautiful sight, and it still makes my heart beat faster when I get back to Manhattan and drive in over the bridge.

We were renting an apartment on the edge of Chelsea. It was pretty small compared to the house in the country. But I had my own room, and I thought it would be okay. Everything was in chaos because the removal men had just dumped boxes and furniture everywhere. My mother had no idea where all the cooking stuff was.

We eventually got the beds sorted out and found a few clothes, then went out to forage for food. As we came in I had been amazed by the buildings rising up all around us, and by how huge the city was. Now we went out and walked a few streets to the East, and every time we crossed an avenue I had to just stand there and stare uptown and downtown, admiring the way the buildings seemed to stretch off into the distance.

The stars were out and all the lights were twinkling in the buildings. It was great. Somewhere around Sixth Avenue we found a nice looking diner and went in for burgers and milkshake (at least that's what I had – I'm not sure about my parents . . .)

I felt so sophisticated sitting there eating in what seemed to me like a fancy restaurant, with all the yellow cabs and buses and huge cars and limos going by outside. And thousands and thousands of people everywhere, even late in the evening. I was totally excited.

I basically never got over it. I still love the city exactly the way I did that first day. My wife has tried to get me to move out to the country a few times, but I'm just a city guy. I love it here. Maybe I'd have reacted differently if I'd grown up here, but coming here at that age impressed on me that New York is an amazing place. I still have that extremely childish reaction to seeing all the shops and people. There's nowhere better in the world.

Dan, 24
Luton, UK

When I was a kid, my mum used to drink too much. I didn't really know that at the time. She used to cry or shout a lot, then she'd drink some more and calm down until she eventually would fall asleep on the sofa or in the hallway of our flat. She split up with my dad when I was about three – I don't even remember him. And I think she had a pretty hard time, but she sometimes wasn't much use as a mother to be honest. She is a lovely woman my mother, but anyone would tell you that maternal instinct doesn't come naturally to her.

But going back to before I really knew all this, there was a day when I was six, in my second year of infants' school. My mum always picked me up after school. She had a lunchtime shift at a restaurant, and then she went home to change out of her uniform, and then came to get me.

But on this day, my mum was nowhere to be seen. Everyone else's mum or dad arrived and the kids were all going home, but I was left alone in on the playground. Eventually Mrs O'Leary, who was the teacher who was on duty, asked me to wait in the office. They tried calling my mum, but they got no response.

Mrs O'Leary eventually talked to the secretary and they asked me who else could look after me. I could only think of my Uncle Jim. They somehow managed to track him down, and about half an hour later he turned up.

He was furious, not at me, but at my mum. He took me home with him for some milk and cake. His wife Sonia was a lovely woman, and was very kind to me, seeing that I wasn't sure what was going on. Then we went to my house. My mum still wasn't answering the phone, but he banged on the door until she came out in her dressing gown.

He immediately started shouting at her and telling her she wasn't fit to look after me, and she started shouting back. It was horrible because all the neighbours came out to see what was happening. Then my mum started crying and sobbing, and they went inside and talked some more.

I went to my room to play. After a while, Jim came to fetch me. My mum was still crying a bit, but she said that they'd agreed that Sonia and Jim were going to look after me for a while. I didn't really mind because I liked them, but then I started crying anyway and that made my mum start again.

Eventually I went with Jim. I lived with him for quite a while, all through that term and most of the summer holidays. My mum used to come and visit, but it was like Jim and Sonia were my parents instead of her. I still consider them to be my parents today.

I did eventually go back to live with her, but I always knew that there was a room for me at Jim's house, and sometimes I needed to know that because my mum was erratic. A lot of the time she was brilliant but she used to get really depressed sometimes, and we ended up working out that at those times it was better if I was with Jim.

What I learned that day was that you can't really depend on anyone, not even your mother. I grew up very quickly because I spent more time looking after my mum than she did looking after me, or at least it sometimes seemed that way. I grew up very calm and able to deal with crises well. But also I think I became quite emotionally distant, because if you can't rely on your mum you withdraw a bit to protect yourself.

I hope it doesn't sound like I'm being unkind to my mother. I do love her, but it's more like she's a scatty sister than a real mother. I was lucky to have Sonia and Jim to give me a bit more stability, but basically I had to learn how to cope with things on my own.

Leon, 36
Ohio

Our house burned down when I was twelve.

I was asleep when the fire started, and my father just ran into the room screaming at me to wake up. There was smoke everywhere, though not many flames. The fire was downstairs at the back of the house, and he had been woken up by the smell, luckily for us.

He didn't wait for me to get up, just grabbed me, threw me over his shoulder and ran down the stair out the front door.

My mother and sister were already outside. My sister was in her Winnie the Pooh pyjamas, and she was crying. She was upset about her toys – she was only six. My dad put me down and went to run back into the house. We were all safe but he wanted to save some papers and things from the front room, but my mother shouted at him not to go.

There was a lot of shouting, as neighbours came out to see what was happening. He was persuaded not to run back in, and it was a good thing, because pretty fast the fire took hold. There were huge flames shooting up through all the windows, and sparks and smoke flying up into the sky.

It was quite a cold night, and the neighbours brought us out some blankets and hot drinks. I was still half asleep, but I remember looking at the burning house and suddenly realizing that all my stuff was gone. My baseball bat, my bike, my clothes, my games . . . everything.

I felt very sad, completely heavy and bad about it. I didn't have any idea what would happen to us. My father kept telling us it would be okay and we were lucky but I didn't feel lucky. I felt awful.

The firemen came and started trying to put the fire out but you could see the house was too far gone. All they were doing was making sure it didn't spread over the yard to the other houses. The neighbour on one side was running around spraying water on his trees and bushes to stop them catching, and I remember my father muttering about how he was only looking out for himself.

The people on the other side were more thoughtful. They looked after us, even took us in that night, giving us cushions and sofas to lie down on, not that any of us slept except my sister, who slept for a few hours then woke up and started crying again.

The day after was truly weird. We went to see the house – it was just a blackened ruin, ashes and fragments. Nothing salvageable. Instead of feeling sad, I felt numb and empty. My dad had arranged for us all to go to his parents so we just said goodbye to the house, got in the car and drove off, leaving everything behind.

His parents lived about 100 miles away, which meant that we were going to have to go to a different school and everything. My sister fell asleep again in the car. The neighbours had given her a doll that had been their mothers' when she was a little girl and she just lay there clinging on to it while we drove in silence.

We never moved back to that town. Apparently my mother had never been too happy there and this was the last straw. We moved back closer to the towns where my parents had grown up, nearer to the rest of our families. My life one day was totally normal, going to school, playing with friends. The next day it was all gone and I was having to start all over in a different place, with new faces and new things to see.

The insurance paid out, though it wasn't as much as it might have been so there were some hard times for us to get through. But we survived. I think that's what that day taught me. You can have everything sorted out the way you think it should be, then suddenly something like a fire takes it all away from you. But you're still the same person – you can adapt and change. I never got my stuff back, but I got new different things in the end.

As I grew up I was never scared to go new places, try different things or leave everything behind. I'd had every-thing taken away from me by that fire and it hadn't killed me, so I always knew I would be okay.

Angela, 26
Melbourne

My life changed when I was only four years old. The frustrating thing about it is that I can only just remember it. My mother died of cancer. I remember her very clearly, playing with me and singing me songs. I could even read a little bit because she had shown me all the letters in the books and had told me how they sounded until I managed to start working out the basic words.

I didn't even know she was ill. Maybe if I'd been older I'd have known. I knew she had to go to hospital a lot and that that was where you went if you were ill, but somehow it didn't connect.

One Friday, my dad picked me up after nursery and took me and my little sister Jenny to stay with my grandmother. Jenny was two, just a toddler, and we often stayed at my grandmothers for a day or so, so I didn't know anything was wrong. I don't remember my grandmother behaving any differently.

My dad didn't come back until Sunday night. I remember that he looked tired. He took me into the garden and told me that my mother had gone away. I just didn't understand. I kept saying, "It's okay, she'll come back later." I only know that because he told me much later. I think it took me a few weeks to understand that she was really gone.

I remember the horrible feeling when I did understand she wasn't coming back. And I remember how quiet my dad was, when he'd always been fun to be around. We stayed at my grandmother's much more from then on, though my father was with us whenever he could be.

24

What still upsets me is that I don't remember the last time I saw her. I must have seen her on the Friday morning. Or maybe she was already in hospital, or had even died already by then? I remember she used to kiss me goodbye. My dad took me to nursery and she would still be in bed, so I'd go in at the last minute and kiss her.

But I'm not sure what happened on that last day or those last few days. I can't ask my dad because it upsets him to talk about that period. He's remarried now, and happily so, which is a good thing. But we don't really talk about it in that much detail.

I like to think I did kiss her goodbye, but I wish I was sure.

Alison, 22
Wicklow, Ireland

This might sound foolish, but I remember one day from my childhood very clearly. As a child I was very much loved and looked after. I had plenty of toys, and I had three elder sisters and brothers who all doted on me. My mother and father never shouted at me except when I knew I was being naughty anyway. It was a very happy childhood, and nothing much happened to upset me. As a result I was quite self-centered. Children all think that the world revolves around them, but maybe when your life is as easy as mine was, that lasts a bit longer.

When I was about seven, I had flu and stayed home from school for a few days. The first few days I was pretty ill and did nothing but lie in bed. Then I got a bit better, and I was sitting up reading and watching the television, knowing that I was actually well enough to go back to school, but enjoying one more day of idleness.

My father used to come home for lunch, because he only worked up the road. When he came home I ran to give him a hug, but he only gave me a quick hug and then started to talk to my mother about something boring.

I ran to get my toy horse, and brought it back to show him something – I'd tied bows in its hair and wanted him to say how clever I was. But he didn't want to look, so I went on and on pestering him, until finally he shouted at me to be quiet. He told me that if I couldn't be quiet and let them to talk to each other I should go to my room.

I ran off crying and went to my room. I sat there, basically waiting for one of them to come and cuddle me, to tell me everything was okay. But they didn't. Then I stopped crying and realized that they were still talking, but that it was quite loud. My mother was shouting about something. I didn't understand, but I know it was something to do with money.

I went out into the hall quietly, and walked back to the kitchen. I remember standing in the doorway watching them. My dad was eating his food, but talking in a very angry voice between mouthfuls. My mother would interrupt him before he could finish, and then they ended up shouting again.

I'm sure they must have argued before then in front of me – they certainly did later on, and they always ended up getting over it and making up. The important thing about this time for me was that for the first time in my life I suddenly realized that my mother and father were real people, that they had their own view of the world, and that I was just one part of it, not the center. It was something to do with the way my father had spoken to me, but more to do with standing there watching them arguing about something I didn't understand and for once seeing that there were other things that were important to them.

This must happen to all children at some age. The reason I feel a bit foolish about it is that it probably happens to most people when they are so young they forget about it quickly. But I was quite old and I still remember the feeling that I was just one small person and that all around me people were living lives, that had nothing to do with me. It's a bit of a scary thought, and a bit of an interesting one. It's something you have to realize to grow up I guess. After that I started watching my brothers and sisters and friends and trying to work out who they were rather than just expecting them to entertain and look after me.

I'm still a bit self-centered today, all my friends tell me so. That's just who I am. Maybe that's why I still remember that day so clearly.

Lily, 33
Toronto

We emigrated from England to Canada when I was seven. My parents had dreams of a whole new life and managed to save up enough to eventually move.

They had been telling me about the move for months, and saying how exciting it was going to be. But I didn't want to go at all. I didn't want to leave all my friends behind and all the things I knew well.

And I didn't want to be so far away from my grandmother and cousins. I found out when I was older that my mother doesn't get on so well with her mother, so she didn't mind leaving the family behind at all, but my grandmother looked after me a lot when I was young, so I was close to her.

They were excited about the move on their own behalves of course, and hoped that I would be as excited as them. But when the day came to go I felt devastated. We had to go and get a very long flight (or it seemed that way to me) and I sulked the whole way.

When we got there it was horribly cold. They'd been telling me how much fun it would be to arrive in the winter and play in the snow, but it was much colder than anything I was used to and I mostly just wanted to stay inside our new house.

After a week or two I started at a new school and found that I couldn't get on with anyone. They tried to make friends with me, but I didn't know what they were talking about half the time. Moving across the ocean is a big culture shock for a seven year old.

I think it took me a long time to recover fully. I don't blame my parents – they were just following their dream. But for me it was difficult. I had been a very sociable child but quickly became withdrawn and didn't have many friends at all. As a result people got the idea I was a snob, so I wasn't too popular at school. Even at high school I was still a bit excluded from everything, although things did get better over time. I made good friends in the end and things were more normal by the time I was a teenager.

I came back to England as soon as I could and lived there for a few years, but actually in the end I understood why my parents had gone in the first place. I came back for a good job in Toronto a few years ago and now I'm happy here, although I may go back to England again if the fancy takes me.

But however things turned out in the end, that day we flew here was a day when everything in my life was suddenly turned upside down. It was a very disorienting experience. Of course worse things happen to people – there are natural disasters and family tragedies far worse than anything I ever had to cope with. But for me moving was a big thing.

Tina, 34
Georgia

My parents split up when I was twelve. They'd always argued a lot, but I guess I never thought they would really give up.

The end came after a week when they had been arguing a lot. I think mostly it was about money. My dad owed my mum some money and she had been counting on getting it back, but he had spent it on something else without telling her. I still don't know all the details – I just remember the arguments.

They had a huge argument on the Friday night. I guess they'd had a drink, and there was a terrible noise of things breaking in the kitchen. I don't know if it was my mother throwing it at my father or just smashing it, but either way a lot of stuff got broken. Me and my brothers knew better than to go and see what was happening. The door eventually slammed and then all we heard was the sound of all the broken glass being cleared up.

In the morning it was only my father at breakfast – he just gave us cereal where my mother would have made pancakes. He told us she had gone away to stay with her sisters for a few days. Actually she had left, but he was hoping she'd come back. It took him the best part of a week to believe she really had gone.

When he finally told us that she had actually left, I was devastated. I'd been very close to her, and had never got on so well with him. I couldn't believe she had left us there with him. He actually coped pretty well – he took over all the cooking and he got together a rota for us to help on the washing and cleaning. It was hard work but we all realized it was a difficult time.

It was three weeks before my mother even phoned. When she did talk to me she kept apologizing and crying and never really managed to explain what was going on. In the end we did start seeing her at the weekends. I had to get a lot older before I understood that my father was actually more stable than her and more able to hold a family together on his own.

She had left us with him because she knew that, but it also hurt her to be away from us. In the very long run it ends up being fun having a mother you see now and then – it's more like having a sister who gives you treats and things, whereas my father always just seemed like a father – unfair, I know, but that's how it is for me.

But the short term was that we had to cope with this massive change. It made us see both of them in a very different light. I started to grow up properly because in that situation I often had to take responsibility for making sure my brothers did their chores, and I had to take on a lot of extra work in the house. It had a big effect on my personality and probably on how I saw relationships once I was a bit older.

I don't blame either of them now. They weren't really suited and it's no wonder they couldn't get along. They're both with other people now and we get along well enough, though I do wonder what it would have been like to grow up in one of those perfect families where nothing ever goes wrong.

Allie, 25
Brooklyn

This will sound very vain, but things totally changed for me the day I finally had my brace taken off from my teeth. I had had one for years, since I was about ten. The orthodontist kept promising that soon we would be able to remove it, and I was desperate for that day to come.

I got teased at school – not really bullied, but ostracized and treated as a dork. It wasn't only because of the brace. These things are always more complicated. But the brace was really bad for my self-confidence, and I felt ugly and self-conscious the whole time I wore it. It was uncomfortable as well, and sometimes it seemed to make me speak a bit strangely – there was a slight lisp, and my "s"s and "f"s came out a bit strangely.

31

The big day eventually arrived. I was thirteen and old enough to be interested in boys and I couldn't wait to stop being "Allie with the metal mouth". The procedure for getting rid of it was pretty quick and the orthodontist said he was happy with how my teeth had turned out. I inspected my mouth in the mirror, with nice straight teeth and no metal in sight. I immediately felt a hundred times better about myself.

My mum was laughing at me because I was so excited, and she took me out to Macy's for a treat, where we bought some silly bracelets and scarves for me to wear. I felt very grown up.

In the end my teen years were fine – the usual problems, but nothing too traumatic. I think that looking back, I overreacted to the brace. I let it affect everything in my life for a while. I've tried to learn from that that even if there is one thing that seems bad in your life, you have to try not to let it cast a cloud over everything. Of course that is easy to say – reality is often more difficult.

But for all that I still feel happy when I remember that lovely feeling of finally having the burden of wearing them taken from me.

Kevin, 34
Wales

I'm not sure that it changed my life, but the day I really remember from when I was young was the day I started school.

I had been looked after by my mother since I was a

baby. She didn't have a lot of friends with children my age, and I was an only child so I led quite a solitary life.

My mother took me in the morning to my new school. I only had to be there for half a day, as it was my first day. She kissed me goodbye, and I clung to her dress. I was really distraught and didn't want her to leave me.

There were some older children laughing at me because I was crying. Then my mother finally left and the teacher took me into the classroom. There were so many other children. I had no idea what to do. It wasn't the start of the school year – it was the summer term, so there were only a few of us new children, and it seemed like everyone knew each other.

A boy called David tried to talk to me – he was new too. But I was really shy and I wouldn't talk to him.

I think I had no idea why I was there. I just thought that if I put up with it my mother would come and get me and I wouldn't have to do that again.

We did all the usual school things, looking at books and playing with bricks, and then my mother came to get me. I told her I didn't like school and I didn't want to go again, but then she told me that all children have to go to school, including me.

That night was probably the most miserable of my life. I felt like I was being put in prison.

The funny thing is that it was all just silly of me. Within a couple of weeks I had made friends – in fact David became my best friend at that school, and I still know him now.

But on a different level I think it did make a difference to me. In my own small way I felt very abandoned by my mother. And I have always had a fear of abandonment in my relationships and friendships.

I think in retrospect I might have always held this against her, until recently anyway. And it's only since I've had children myself that I've really seen it from her point of view.

She felt she was doing the best thing by looking after me herself. In fact she was giving me all the love she could. But that made it hurt more when I thought that her love was being withdrawn.

I didn't suffer because of any of this – I had a comfortable childhood and no real problems. I just find it interesting looking back, that moment of being left of school still feels so traumatic.

My mother was quite a remote cold person, and it took me a long time to understand that she expresses her love in a more indirect way than many people. Now I have nothing but respect for her, and I try to bring my own children up in the best way I can.

But one thing I did do differently from my mother was I made sure that my kids had other children their own age to play with at an early age. I think it's really important because it makes them learn how to socialize. My kids have all gone to playgroups or nurseries at an early age, which I hope has helped them when they transferred to school.

Having said that, who knows what I have done wrong? You try your best to get everything right, and then no doubt one day, twenty years from now, something will come out in analysis and one of them will come home to tell me exactly how I ruined their lives!

I really hope not though. Children seem very resilient

but actually they are fragile and learn from everything that happens to them. You can't completely protect them all the time, but you have to try your best.

Moments of Inspiration

Sometimes a life can be changed by one single thought or idea. But when a flash of inspiration strikes, we aren't always in a position to be able to act on it.

An idea can become an aim or target in life, something that shapes the way that we want to be and to live our lives. Some of the accounts here deal with someone's first artistic inspiration – the idea of becoming a ballerina for instance. Others deal with business ideas, moments of inspiration that created a new opportunity for the person who had the idea.

In some cases we can act immediately on inspiration. When Mario discovered Elvis, he could immediately seek out more information on his new fascination, and this had a longer term effect on his life.

In other cases a moment of inspiration shapes longer-term events – when Andrew decided to change his lifestyle, he wasn't at that stage in a position to achieve this. But through persistence and long term planning he was able to make his dream come true. For Hailey, the inspiration really comes from outside – she was simply performing her job to the best of her abilities when someone else spotted her potential. But this only came about because of the attitudes she brought to her everyday life.

One moral I take from these stories is that while we can often pinpoint a moment our life changed, there is often a bigger picture evolving in the background. Maria left her workplace in a way that seems quite sudden. But clearly she had been reflecting on her situation in life for a while and one day this all crystallized in such a way as to allow her to make a life-changing decision.

So while the central theme that links these accounts is inspiration, they also carry the moral that your whole life often feeds into a small moment, which is the catalyst for change. If you live your life in such a way as to allow for the possibility of change and learning, then you keep your mind open to the possibilities that may come your way.

And if you live each day as though it might be a day that changes your life, then perhaps that also makes it more likely that one day your life will change more dramatically than you expected. Even when you life changes for the worse, it is important to be able to deal with the consequences, as it has never helped anyone to live in the past. But lives constantly change both for the better and for the worse in tiny incremental ways. Later on we may or may not be able to identify the exact moment when something changed, but sometimes, as with these stories, it just may be that we can.

Mario, 67
Florence

The first time I heard Elvis Presley sing was a big day in my life. I grew up in a little village not so far from Florence, and most of the music we had at home was the traditional Italian music that was everywhere at that time. I heard American music sometimes, and it was not bad but nothing special – all those big bands and crooners. Sometimes you would hear songs that were translations of Italian songs and they always seemed passionless and weak.

But when I heard Elvis as a teenager, it was really something. It was in a café in town. I'd gone with my mother and she was off shopping while I fetched a few things I needed. I was going to meet her at the café, where Elvis came on the radio – *Baby Let's Play House*. He sounded completely alien and produced a weird gargling sound as though it was all a bit out of control – but at the same time it was thrilling.

It wasn't just about music for me, it was about changing the way I saw the world. I had very cosy, parochial views about how Italy was the only place in the world and how Italian culture was superior. Then here came this astonishing noise, and more rock and roll followed, which showed me that there was something vibrant and extraordinary happening in America of all places. I started to seek out more rock and roll records and in the process discovered blues records, which I became very fond of. Through the research I had to do to track this music down, I found out a lot more about the world beyond my village – and became fascinated by it. As a result I started to long to travel and rather than spend any money I had, I saved so that I could go away. To start with I travelled Europe and managed to get to amazing places like the Greek Islands for next to nothing, just hitching and sleeping in a tent.

Later I managed to get to America, and even out to the Far East. I did all sorts of things in my twenties and thirties – the first real inspiration for me to discover the world came from that weird voice coming over the radio, like a transmission from outer space.

Hank, 43
Scotland

I'm a writer now. I make my living by writing for magazines and whoever will take my work. I've even had a novel published though it hasn't sold many copies.

But I used to be a professional criminal. I grew up in a very rough area, and from a young age I was involved in drug dealing and robbery. When you start that young it just becomes a way of life. I got caught often enough and so spent years in prison. I saw it as a price you had to pay for an easy life on the outside, and so I did the time without worrying about it.

During my third prison sentence I was trying to persuade the warders that I was ready for parole, so I went to a poetry workshop. Not my sort of thing at all, but it all goes down on your record, and the more co-operative you are over these little things, the more ready they are to let you out early.

But the workshop was actually quite interesting. The man running it wasn't quite the poncy middle class type I was expecting. He hadn't ever been in prison himself, but he had come from a similar background to me. And he was a poet. He read us some of his poems, and they meant something to me in a way that poetry never had before. Basically because they were about the sorts of things I understood: Friday nights in the pub, benefit fraud, or having a fight.

I asked him some questions and said, why would anyone want to read these poems. No one is interested in the lives of people like us. He said I was wrong and that actually middle class people like nothing better than the feeling that they are reading something really authentic and gritty. He said that if you have lived a real hard life, you are inherently more interesting to the people who actually read books.

I liked his attitude. He kind of knew that he was being patronized by some of the people who read his work or bought it. But at the same time, he was getting something out of it.

I was literate. I could read and write reasonably well. But it had simply never occurred to me that it was a useful skill. But to be honest I was getting tired of being in prison. I wanted to live a more normal life, and meeting that writer gave me the idea I could do something different in life. I didn't really expect it to work, but I was lucky and got a few things published in magazines. Even before I left prison – I sent them articles about what it was like on the inside, and they got published.

That's how I managed to give up the life I had been

living until them. So that poetry workshop was a big thing for me. I never wrote a single poem, but even so it changed my life.

Dale, 50
New South Wales

When I was in my twenties I used to deal in second hand cars. My uncle had been a car dealer and he had taught me the ropes. He used to take me to auctions with him in Sydney and elsewhere, and taught me how to find cars for less than their value, make them look worth more, and sell them on as quick as possible. I'd learned all this stuff by the time I was twenty and I figured that was how I'd make a living. It seemed as good a life as any other. I was a good mechanic and that made life easier.

So I set up in my hometown as a dealer. I got a few cars together, and hired a yard to keep them in with a garage for doing some work. I had a loan from my uncle and a bit more from the bank, and I thought I'd be fine.

The thing was, that town wasn't such a great place to deal in. It took me a while to work it out, but basically it was a bit too pretentious. A lot of people wanted to buy new cars. Other people liked to buy direct from someone who had owned the car. A lot of people weren't keen on buying from a dealer. I sold cars, but not fast enough, and the bills started to mount up. I was starting to think I was going to get in real money trouble because I was having trouble meeting my monthly repayments on the bank loan.

One day a man was in my yard looking at a car. He gave it a good going over but in the end it looked like he was going to leave it. I asked him what he needed it for and he told me that it was just an extra car for the family. He and his wife had cars that their children borrowed at the weekend. But sometimes there were arguments when he would be away for the weekend and someone wouldn't get to use the car. So he wanted a spare for the kids to argue over. But he wasn't sure he wanted to lay out the money.

I said it sounded like he just needed an occasional car, one he could borrow rather than buy. And for some reason something clicked in my mind. I thought that maybe I could set up a sideline renting cars. I asked him if he'd be interested in this option and he said maybe. But the town didn't have a single car hire place. The nearest was about fifty miles away. So I got a bit excited about it and looked into all the legal stuff (quite complicated but I was determined). And within a few weeks I had the first car hire firm that town had ever seen. And it made me twenty times more money than the dealing ever had. It was just the right idea for the right town at the right time. A year or so after that I set up a taxi firm too. There was already another in town, but I made sure my drivers were all polite and helpful and we won a lot of business very quickly.

It all came from one little wave of inspiration, but I changed my whole idea of how to run my business, and from that I built my way up to a much more successful life.

Andrew, 40
Cumbria, England

I used to play guitar in a band. We were based in London, but we spent a lot of time travelling around the country touring. We did a few tours abroad as well, which were always exciting, but most of it was just driving round and round Britain in the same old transit van.

Touring is essentially very boring. You get up in some hotel or bed and breakfast, drive half the day to another dodgy venue, soundcheck, try to find some cheap food which isn't too bad (I ate a lot of curry and chips in those days). Then the gig, which is either good or bad. If it's good, then you have a great time, but it only lasts about an hour. The other twenty-three hours of the day are just there to be got through. And if the gig is bad the whole thing feels like a waste of time.

Occasionally we used to have a journey where there was enough time to stop off somewhere. If (a big if) we could all agree, we might take an hour or so to walk around an interesting town, or to see somewhere in the country.

The day I remember the best was when we were driving from a gig in Edinburgh to the gig the next day in Manchester. There are various faster ways of doing the route, but for some reason the driver wanted to divert through Cumbria. This meant we took the road over the Pennines towards Penrith, on the edge of the Lake District. We had plenty of time so we stopped on top of the hill for a break. I walked about ten minutes away from the van, up hill, and reached the edge of a steep slope down. It was an amazing sight. It was a beautiful clear April day, and the

46

whole Eden valley was down beneath me – a beautiful English landscape. Over in the distance I could see a lake, I'm not sure which one, but it was very big, and beyond that the snowy peak of a mountain. And looking down the hill I saw what I thought was a rabbit running across the slope. But I realised as I watched it was actually a hare – they're beautiful to watch, and I've only seen one a few times since, so I took it as a kind of omen.

Then I went back to the van and we drove down to the bottom of the hill, where we stopped for lunch in a lovely little village called Melmerby, which had an amazing bakery and also a great local pub. I remember sitting there thinking that my life in London was just too much hassle, and that what I actually wanted from life was to live somewhere simple and beautiful like this.

And it became my goal to make that happen. I was in the band for another year or two, but I started building up a design business for myself. All the time I was aiming to get to a position where I could work for myself freelance, and it wouldn't matter if I was in a city or not. It took a few more years, but eventually I had a real business going, and a bit of money saved up so I drove up here and stayed in a room at the pub in Melmerby while I looked around for somewhere to live. I ended up staying for a while in Appleby, which is not far away, and then living a bit closer to Penrith but right out in the country in a cottage. The building needed a lot of work when I moved in, so between that and the design I was extremely busy. But it is such a beautiful part of the world, close to the lakes and the hills, and completely peaceful.

I'm proud of myself because I gave myself a goal, and

then kept working and working at it until I got to where I wanted to be. And now I'm here I can say that it was definitely worth all the work.

Hailey, 32
Washington

I used to work in a children's bookstore. It wasn't well paid, but I enjoyed it. I wasn't especially ambitious, although I sometimes felt that I was at a bit of a dead end in my life.

One day a guy in a suit came in. I asked if I could help him and he explained that he was looking for a present for his daughter, who was eight. He seemed like someone quite wealthy who maybe didn't get that much time at home, and he seemed very uncertain what sorts of things his daughter liked. I only found out later that the daughter actually lived with his ex-wife, which explains that.

I took him through a lot of the possibilities in the store. I found him books that an eight year old might like, and explained all the stories to him (I used to spend a lot of time reading the books when it was quiet). Then I went through all the toys, and the make-up kits and so on in the toy department.

He was not sure what to get. Then he got a mobile phone call and had to leave very quickly, so he didn't buy anything after all that.

He came back a few days later, and told me that he had decide on one of the hairdressing sets I had been showing him. The only problem was that it had sold out since he had called. He was so dismayed, I promised him to try and get another. I had to call about five different wholesalers, and none of them had one. Then finally I found someone who could deliver to us the following Tuesday.

I gave Mr Wallace (he had given me his details for this) a call, and it turned out that he was going to be out of town, and it was his daughter's birthday the following week.

He asked me if I could possibly arrange to send it – he sent me a letter for her, and I put this in with a card and wrapped the present – all charged to him of course.

The following week I was pottering about tidying shelves in the bookshop when Mr Wallace appeared again. First of all he thanked me effusively for all the help with the present – I'd chosen it, found it and sent it for him, and he couldn't thank me enough.

He then rather unexpectedly went on to ask if I would be interested in going and working for him. It turns out that he runs a rather large distribution company. He had been trying to get an assistant for a while and kept being disappointed. He told me I would have to do an interview, but that if it all went well he really wanted to see if I could do it. Basically he said that he only liked employees who were prepared to go the extra mile and to really take on and solve problems rather than passing the buck and trying to avoid responsibility. He said that the way I had dealt with him and his problem had made him suddenly wonder if I could be as efficient at dealing with his customers and contacts.

I was amazed, as I had only meant to be helpful. But the more I thought about it the more I thought that it was time for a new challenge in my life, so I went along for a chat later that week, and at the end of the month ended up working for him.

It was a complete change – from low-pressure to high-pressure, casual to smart, easygoing to high achieving. But I enjoyed it. I think I had been coasting along for too long, and once I got this new opportunity, found it was something I could really get my teeth into.

It was only two years before I got promoted and now I work as commercial director for the same company. I still don't really know what it was about me that made him pick me out and ask me to help, but I'm glad it happened. The only moral I can take from this is that you need to treat even everyday situations as though they might change your life. Imagine if he had come in that day and I had been surly and rude, or had not bothered to chase down those suppliers. I'd have still been going along the same, and I'd never even have known about the amazing opportunity I had wasted!

Maria, 30
Paris

I had quite a high-powered job, working for an advertising agency. I had taken a few years working my way up from the bottom, and I was proud of what I had achieved. But I don't think I was very happy. The office was full of backstabbing. People would do anything to gain an advantage or get the account, and there was no real personal loyalty.

But I wasn't consciously unhappy. I had adjusted to

working in that environment and I had my friends and allies within the company.

One day there was a problem with one of the accounts. The campaign was getting received badly by focus groups and the advertiser was getting cold feet about going ahead with us. I had worked on the campaign with a colleague.

We had a meeting, the two of us with our manager. I was very angry because my colleague was in a very sneaky way trying to transfer any blame for the problem away from her and on to me. I was trying to share the blame and be honest but the result was that my manager was given the impression that it was my fault that there was a problem. I have no difficulty in taking responsibility for a mistake, so I didn't mind that at all. But I did mind watching her trying to evade responsibility in that way very much.

I left the building at lunchtime, meaning to think things over and work out how best to deal with the situation – should I confront her privately, or find a different way of dealing with things? Or should I just leave things as they were?

I went to a restaurant near the Bastille, a local brasserie that I was very fond of. I ate alone and started thinking. But instead of thinking about the immediate problem I started thinking about my whole situation in life. What was I doing in this profession where people behaved that way? It all seemed so pointless and despicable.

Instead of leaving to go back to the office, I stayed on and had another coffee and a dessert. And then I had another coffee. I hadn't actually made a decision. But I knew that I didn't want to go back right then. In fact I didn't want to go back at all.

The more I thought about it, the more I became convinced that there was something wrong with my whole life and that I couldn't fix it unless I left that job.

Still I thought I might go back. Several times I pushed my chair back meaning to go, thinking that I might resign. But I was very reluctant to do so, and finally it came to me that the easiest thing would be simply never to go back.

So that's what I did. I left the brasserie and walked down towards the river instead. I walked home along the river, and I felt wonderful at leaving all my worries behind.

I went home and had a long bath and then called a friend to come over with a bottle of wine. We talked and talked and I had a fine evening. The next day there were a lot of messages on my telephones, but I didn't care. I never called them to explain. That seems a bit bad in retrospect but it was a total clean break for me. I went and got myself a job in a local shop for a while to survive, and concentrated on working out what I should do next.

I won't tell the whole story of how I got from there to here, but it was the best thing I have ever done. It was a little terrifying, as up until then I had been so wrapped up in the identity of being in that profession, but giving it all up gave me a chance to start with a blank slate. I was able to concentrate on what I wanted to do and be in my life, and I am much the better for it today in every possible way.

Ellis, 44
New Hampshire

I was in Boston to meet my friend Al. We were supposed to meet up in a café that he had chosen. But in the interim the place had gone out of business and was all boarded up.

So we walked a couple of blocks to find somewhere else. There was an unusual place, which was a mixture of a gift store and a coffee place. Al used to have a gift store so he was interested in going in to look around.

It turned out to be a lovely experience. They had really good coffee and a selection of marvellous cakes. It was simple but excellent and the service was perfect.

We started talking about life and it turned out that both of us were a bit bored of the jobs we were doing. He looked around him and said that what he'd really like would be to run somewhere like this.

I don't know why, but I just said "Well, why don't we?" Now I've known Al since we were at college, but we'd never in any way talked about going into business together. But at that moment it seemed like such a simple, good idea. We get on in exactly the right way. We are completely blunt and honest with each other. We get on well on a day-to-day basis, even though we are not the closest friends in the world. It seemed like we could get on in a way that would work in business.

So we started to talk about it, and do the math. There was a vacant store in my town that looked promising – he lives about fifty miles out in the country, but he didn't mind doing the travelling. And after a lot of hesitation and uncertainty, we took the property.

Let me tell you it was not simple. We worked really hard to get the place ready. Things went wrong right from the start. We had a flood in the kitchen, and one of our suppliers went bust the week we started, losing us money in the process. We got down close to our last reserves of cash at one point.

But from the start we got some good custom, and we always felt that we could make it work. After the teething problems, we started to get on top of the situation and little by little we turned it around and made it a success.

We didn't always get on, but we were always honest about any problems and we always treated each other with respect, which I think is what you need to do.

After about five years we looked around and realized we had a success on our hands. We had enough money to open a second branch in the next town. And then another and another. We had one or two failures, but now we have a chain of ten stores. They are not branded, each one is a unique place. But we have the financial freedom we always wanted and a lifestyle that is always interesting, varied and satisfying. And all that came from an accidental cup of coffee!

Anya, 28
Paris

My grandmother took me to the ballet when I was five, when we still lived in Moscow (my family are Russian, but we moved away when I was ten). She wasn't sure I would be old enough to understand it. Before hand she spent a lot of time telling me over and over that I had to be quiet and not talk and only clap when she did. But she shouldn't have worried because from the start of the show I was completely entranced.

The curtains opened and the scene was a beautiful palace, with silk drapes and gold furniture, and from there in I couldn't look away. It was a fairy tale for me. The whole place, with comfortable velvet seats, and all the men and women dressed in magnificent clothes – the ladies in beautiful dresses. It was so unlike everything in everyday life.

And the ballerinas were perfect – so graceful and pretty in their lovely costumes. I didn't really understand the story – my grandmother had to explain it to me afterwards. But I sat quietly enjoying every minute anyway.

As soon as we came out of the theatre I told my grandmother I wanted to be a ballerina when I grew up. She laughed, as grandmothers do – I'm sure children are always saying they want to be an astronaut or a train driver or whatever. But I absolutely meant it, and I never forgot that that was what I wanted to do. I spent years nagging my grandmother into taking me to the ballet whenever I could, and found out everything I could about it. It was only after we came to Europe that I was able to have dance lessons, but I was very focused and I ended up living out my childhood dream. It's a long story and I won't tell you all of it, but I have danced some lovely roles with a terrific company in cities around the world. Now I am hoping to continue working within the ballet as a choreographer. But if my grandmother hadn't taken me to see the show that day my life might have turned out very differently.

Linda, 38
New Jersey

When I was thirty, I was very overweight. After I had my kids I kind of gave up on myself, and piled on the pounds. But then after one Christmas I saw pictures of myself and hardly recognized that big fat girl in the photos, so finally I became determined to lose the excess.

I turned out to be good at dieting, once I really put my mind to it. I lost ninety pounds in nine months. I did it through a combination of sheer determination, setting myself reasonable targets, persisting when the results were disappointing and always allowing myself one or two tiny treats so that I didn't feel completely hopeless. Eventually I got back down very close to the weight I had been before the kids.

I felt 100% better about myself. Also because the kids were all at school now, I was starting to think about going back to work – that had been another motivation for me. I felt that employers would take me less seriously while I was overweight. That may be unfair, but I think it is true nonetheless.

But even with my new confidence I was finding it a bit hard to get a job. Employers worry about you when you have been looking after children for so long. I don't know why – it's ridiculous when you have been coping with so much at home to think you can't manage to do a little job, but that's the attitude you meet as a returning mother.

One of my friends came round one day. She was a little overweight, though not by as much as I had been. Over a cup of coffee she asked me if I could help her with some advice on how to lose the weight. She said that I had done it so amazingly, and so calmly, that she felt like I must know some magic way of losing weight. I told her how I had done it – the hard work, the targets, the little treats and the never giving up because of bad news.

She went away that week and tried to do what I had said, and by the end of the first week she had lost two pounds. She called me up to thank me, and said, you ought to do this for other people because you're so good at it.

And that's the little comment that made me realize I had a real opportunity. I was struggling to find work, but there was something I was very good at that I could teach. I had the photographic proof of how much weight I had lost, and that would help.

I spent the weekend putting together a business plan, and once I was sure I knew what I wanted to do I borrowed a couple of hundred dollars from the bank to make some publicity material. I had decided to set up a slimming class, where women could come on a weekly basis to share their slimming stories and to try and achieve more because they were working together.

Of course it's not a new idea by any means – others have done it, and there was already one rival class in my town. But I had never considered doing it, and I felt sure that if I got off to a good start I would be able to make a go of it.

The other thing I did was to research all the towns in a hundred mile radius to find towns where there wasn't a local class. I figured that if I was prepared to put the time in, travelling to hand out leaflets and then to give a regular class, I might do better if I spread the net wider.

This was the most successful part of the new business. I got together a small class in my town, and learned a lot from running that for a few months. But once I got the classes in other towns going, it really took off.

There were at least five towns where no one had done this recently, so there was a real customer base waiting for me, and some of those classes were the biggest I did.

Within a year I was doing well enough to start delegating some of the classes to the better students. Women who had really lost weight with me would take over teaching, and keep the class going while I took a cut.

By the end of the year I had classes going all over the state – it was a real business with an office and everything. And all that came from one little comment my friend made to me. I took her on holiday last year as a belated thank you.

Sal, 55
Minnesota

Five years ago I won the lottery. It's not quite as dramatic as it sounds – we had a syndicate at work, and I won a thirty-fifth part of three million dollars. About eighty thousand dollars. Which is quite a lot, but it's not like I could buy a mansion and live the life of a millionaire.

Everyone was so excited when we won the money, we were all dancing around at work, and quite a few people came in the next Monday with beautiful new cars. No one gave up work – it wasn't that much money. But everyone was pleased that they would have that bit of extra money for luxuries.

I didn't know what to do with the money. Our mortgage was nearly paid off, and so I paid the last twenty thousand of it, and that made my husband happy. But we weren't so poor anyway once we'd done that, and there weren't any particular things I wanted to spend the money on.

I had a few people being a bit weird with me, which was interesting – sneering at me for being mean, or acting like I was putting on some kind of an act. It's funny how people behave when money is about.

I had a party for my family a few weeks after the win, and it was wonderful – there were four generations there – my parents, our children and grandchildren, all in one place.

And at the party I suddenly realized what I really wanted to do with the money. I talked to a few people and everyone liked the idea, so I went away and organized it.

The summer afterwards we had a huge family holiday in Mexico – all of the family came – twenty-five people. It was absolutely wonderful. All these people who I usually only see for an hour or so were all in one place for two weeks. In some ways that was the time I really had to get to know people in my family. We all work so hard that we never get a long time to spend with each other. But on holiday I had long conversation with all my children's partners, and with all the grandchildren. We had the most lovely relaxing time.

Some people have told me that I blew the money doing that, but I feel that it was the most positive thing I could do. It brought our family together in a very definite way, and it gave me a memory I will treasure until the day I die. What more can you do with money?

Times of Crisis

We live in a strange period of history. Recent events such as the Asian tsunami, Hurricane Katrina, the flooding of New Orleans, and 9/11 have made us more conscious than ever of the possibility of a sudden catastrophic event that, in a moment, changes thousands of lives irrevocably. Whether man-made, as with a terrorist attack, or natural, as in the floods, storms and earthquakes that seem increasingly common, which of us has not thought about how they would react if caught up in such an event?

But times of crisis come on different scales. Events of global and political significance affect individuals in a wide variety of ways. At the same time, people are dealing with their own everyday catastrophies. Houses that are lost to natural accidents, marriages that break down, bankruptcy, the loss of a job: these are all events that impact in serious ways upon our lives.

Much of the interest for me in the accounts that follow is to consider the ways that people react to the crises that envelope their lives. Some react with indefatigable purpose. Others become depressed and find it hard to escape from the problems that ensue. Yet others learn from their own mistakes and vow to move on.

When we are subject to tragic or difficult events, do we shake our fists at fate in defiance, or do we meditate on our small place in the world, and try to recover to survive until another day?

63

If I put myself in the places of the people who wrote these accounts, I find it very hard to say what reaction I would have. For some such as Karena and Anton, the political events which they describe had also defined their lives in previous years, so the liberations they describe are hard to fully comprehend without having lived through the same oppressions.

But in the cases of those whose everyday lives, relationships and jobs came under severe strain as a result of the events described, we can all imagine similar events in our own lives. I don't know how I would react, but I can only hope I would be able to show the dignity and comprehension of my circumstances that is personified in so many of these accounts.

Peter, 44
Switzerland

Ten years ago I was living what I thought was a happy life in Bonn, in Germany. I was married to a beautiful girl, and we had a group of friends we had known for a long time.

Then one day I came home from work early and found my wife in bed with one of my closest friends, Frederick, someone I also worked with on a daily basis in my business. There was no possibility of forgiving this and getting on with things – it was too much of a betrayal. Apparently it had been going on for some time.

She moved in with Frederick and I tried to get on with life. The difficulty was that my whole life was now tainted by this problem. I worked with Frederick so everyone at work knew about it, and had to try to deal with the two of us in a way that would not be too disruptive. And even if I managed to get through the day at work, my group of friends was splitting into people who would talk to me, and people who would talk to them. The whole process of taking sides is very painful – you have difficult phone calls where people won't quite say what they mean, but you have to read between the lines. In addition, several of these so-called friends had known about the affair while it was happening and had done nothing to stop it or to let me know, so my friendships with them were tainted in any case.

I actually tried to live my normal life for about six months. Then one day, instead of going to work I went for a drive out of town. I went to a bit of the country I know well and went for a long walk by myself through the forest.

I thought about everything in my life, and tried to work out how to keep the good things and leave behind the bad. And it gradually dawned on me as I walked that everything I thought of as good in my life was attached to something bad – friends who talked to me, but still saw the friends who talked to my wife and Frederick. Work things, favourite places, restaurants, shops, all linked together in painful ways. Even my family, who I love dearly, were difficult as they couldn't help but show that they were sad that we had split up. Even this forest I was walking in was somewhere I had been with her in happier times.

To start with that made me feel very bad. But then I started to consider what my options were, and I wondered what it would be like to leave absolutely everything behind. And the more I thought about that the more light and free I felt. The more I realized that the only way of really sorting out problems at this stage was to leave them all behind. I knew I might have to come back later, but if so it would be on my own terms.

So I drove back and went into work. I gave all my contracts notice that I was leaving town and that while I would see out all existing work, I wouldn't be taking any more on. I worked like a dog to get all of my commitments fulfilled because I would not have felt happy to go any other way. Meanwhile at home I packed up all my things.

I took this all to something of an extreme. I put all of my possessions into storage, except some that I just threw away. I traded my old car for a new cheaper one, as I needed all my money. And I even left my clothes behind. I went to a shop the day before I left and bought three sets of very basic clothes, all new, that I could take with me.

And then I closed up my apartment, took the keys back to the landlord, and drove away with absolutely nothing in the car except those new sets of clothes.

It felt wonderful. I had no idea where I was going, but my first thought was to drive down through Europe to the mountains and the Mediterranean, so I set off heading south and decided to see where I would end up. I slept in the car as often as not, and for a few months I just did whatever I felt like. I was like complete renewal, where everything in my past life fell away from me. And all the things that had seemed so overwhelming and sad suddenly seemed small and faraway.

Eventually of course I had to get a job and put down some roots – I worked in a bar down in Nice for a while, then I met up with some new people, and eventually ended up here in Geneva. I have a new life, different friends and a different career, and I'm very happy. I don't think I could have come so far so quickly without leaving everything behind.

I did actually go home for a visit about five years ago, and it was pleasant to see people, especially my family. But it didn't make me feel that I had done the wrong thing at all.

Don, 41
Leeds

A few years ago now I had been having a lot of money problems. The house I was in had fallen in value, so I had a bad case of negative equity. Then I split up with my girlfriend and lost my job. I got a new job but it paid less and I had lost a couple of months wages along the way. On top of that I had been charging everything to credit cards, and the bills started to mount up in a really bad way. Everytime I got paid most of it would go on to the cards, loans and the mortgage, but then any money I needed to live off was putting me further into debt – all I was ever doing was paying off the interest and then getting into debt.

It simply couldn't go on like that. I went to a debt advisor, but it was much too late by then. He did help me by coming to agreements with all my creditors whereby they froze the balances on the loans and agreed to a longer payment period. But I couldn't even keep to that. I took out a new consolidation loan, and that pushed me over the edge within a month or two. I finally couldn't make the mortgage payments.

It all sounds so simple, but this was a period of constant stress, denial and worry. I knew things were terrible, but I still never really got a grip and stopped spending. Right to the end I would go out at the weekend and buy a treat on my credit card because I needed cheering up. The banks don't help as they keep on increasing your limit over and over until you have far too much credit. Then, when it becomes a problem it is already an insurmountable one. I owed the equivalent of a year's salary, and now the bank was not willing to renegotiate on the mortgage.

I had no option but bankruptcy. These days people seem to think bankruptcy is an easy option, but there was a real stigma attached to it then. In fact I think even now people don't realize how humiliating it will be to go through the process. I basically lost everything, – the house, the car, my self-respect and had to move home with my parents at the age of thirty-one. Of course I was grateful to them for taking me back in but I felt like such a fool.

The real day that everything came to a head was the day I had to give the keys back to the bank. I had cleared out everything I still had, and the house was just empty with a few boxes of junk and rubbish in the corners. It was a heartbreaking moment.

And then you don't have proper banking facilities or anything. I still had my job, but I had to live rigidly within my means, and some of my creditors were receiving payments from my salary so the amount I had to survive on was tiny.

The bankruptcy was eventually discharged, after years of hard work. I still haven't bought another house, but I rent and my life is back to something like normal. But I did learn a massive lesson, even if it was a bit late in life. Now I am careful with money. I have credit cards (they just throw them at you these days, whatever your history), but I pay them off monthly. I use credit for large items, but only in a very careful way – I budget exactly how I am going to pay them back. There is no easier path to bankruptcy than spending money you don't know how to pay back, and I will never make that mistake again.

Keith, 28
Aberdeen

My family's house was destroyed in a gas explosion when I was thirteen. It was about two in the morning when we were woken up by this huge commotion. It wasn't so much a bang as a kind of thump, the physical feeling of being pushed. I fell out of bed somehow, and the windows were all blown in. I had no idea what was going on. There was a sound of breaking glass falling everywhere, and then my mum shouting to see if everyone was okay. Luckily, none of us got hurt, although my father had a cut to his hand, where it had been outside the bed and he had been hit by some glass. He had a shirt wrapped around it. But the lights didn't work and some of the doors were hard to open. We had to kick my sister's door down to get her out. Then we ran outside in our pajamas, with a blanket or two.

The house next door was pretty much gone. That was where the explosion had been. The remnants of it were burning. There were already fire engines on the way, we could hear them, and some of the neighbours were out in the street. They were semi-detached houses so it was only ours which had been directly damaged, though a few other windows were damaged too.

Someone was calling for Mrs Adams who lived there. She was a pensioner who lived on her own. But you could see right away there was no chance she was alive. The house was destroyed and all the rubble was in a terrible scattered pile through the garden.

Around this point my mum started crying un-controllably, and I found I was shaking really badly. It's funny that when it actually happened we were all very calm, but once we went outside we became a bit panicky.

To start with, it looked as though our house might be okay. But the more you looked, the more you could see that it had been damaged. The connecting wall was exposed, and it was tilting, and a part of the roof had been blown out. The real damage wasn't apparent, but the lower part of the structure had been damaged so badly that there was no solution except to demolish both houses together.

No one ever found out what happened. Mrs Adam maybe fell asleep with the fire on or something, but the firemen couldn't be sure. She didn't seem to have any relatives, and there was a quiet funeral, which we went to, even though we hadn't known her well.

We stayed with my aunt and uncle for a while. It turned out that the insurance my dad had on the house was nowhere near enough to get us the same standard of living we had enjoyed. We weren't rich but we had a comfortable middle-class lifestyle. But somehow the insurance turned out to be enough only to buy an old terrace in town and we struggled to pay for furniture and clothes and all the necessities of life.

I think my mother blamed my father for this, and he blamed himself but became quite bitter about it. He started drinking more and they would argue when he came home from a night out. They had always been fine together, but the strain of this sudden change affected their marriage badly for a while.

It was a very strange few years. I moved out once I was sixteen, and my sister followed soon after. We loved our parents, but those last few years had been very strange for us. All our certainties and assumptions about life had suddenly been tossed aside, and we had been plunged into a quite different world.

It was maybe a good lesson to learn about how conditional everything is in life. You have to fight for what you have, and struggle to protect and preserve the good things in life because they matter. That's the way I saw it, and so did my sister. We both became very driven in our teens and early twenties, and succeeded at finding good careers for ourselves.

The funny thing is my mother and father got completely over their bad patch in the end. The old terrace in town ended up gaining in value – they lived there quite happily for a while once we had moved out and it was less crowded. The area became gentrified as the middle class and students bought up terraces or "urban cottages" as they like to call them, and they ended up moving back out to a semi-detached house not so far from where the first house had been destroyed.

In the end it is almost as though nothing happened for them, whereas for me and my sister it was something of a turning point in life. Perhaps that's just the age we were at, on the edge of our teens, where such upheaval makes a very deep impression on you.

Angie, 26
Denver

No one believes me when I tell them this story but it's absolutely true. When my baby Ruth was born I had no idea I was pregnant!

I was only a kid, seventeen years old. I knew about the facts of life and everything of course, and yes I did know how you get pregnant, though me and my boyfriend had taken precautions and so I had no reason to think anything had happened.

I didn't put on that much weight. I'm slightly on the big

side anyway, so maybe it was easier not to notice. I don't remember being sick at all. But I did have pains in my stomach, and there was a bit of blood at times. I was vaguely worried that there might be something wrong in there but I kept putting it out of my mind.

Some people say that if this happens it's just denial. That deep down you know you are pregnant, but you are deceiving yourself. Well I don't know how you would go about deceiving yourself. I mean if you are lying to yourself you know the truth, right? But that just wasn't how it was with me. It was wintertime, I had a few colds, I put on a few pounds, and every now and then my stomach felt a bit weird.

In February I started to feel a bit strange in another way. It was kind of fluttering in my chest. I was actually having a bit of a strange time as I'd been arguing with my mother and I'd moved in with my boyfriend, so I thought it was just anxiety or something.

Then one day I started getting these pains, real bad pains. I was doubled up in pain on my bed and I had to call my boyfriend Leon to come and get me. He took me to hospital. There was a very severe nurse there, and she gave me a quick examination. She asked me how long gone I was. I didn't even know what she was talking about. She just rolled her eyes and went and got a doctor.

He came and he was much nicer. He gave my stomach a good prod. I was almost screaming every time these pains came along now. He told me that I was having a baby, and that I was in labour.

Leon just about fainted with shock. I've never seen someone go that pale before. He had to sit down to get over it. I just lay there with my mouth open, amazed I hadn't realized. As soon as he said I was pregnant I put it all together in my mind and it made sense. I still couldn't work out what had happened but as the doctor said, no contraception is 100% reliable, so it was just bad luck.

I told Leon he had to call my mother for me, and he walked out looking like a ghost. I stood up to try and lean over to ease the pain and that's when the waters broke, so there wasn't any doubt at all left in my mind.

My mother arrived about forty minutes later, just as I was getting into the final stages. The first thing she did was walk in shouting at Leon and me for being so dumb. But once she saw me there she just melted and held my hand tight. She was my mother after all, and this was her first grandchild.

It hurt, and it took a long time, but eventually the baby arrived. They asked me what I was going to call it, and I said how in hell did I know, I didn't even know about her until a couple of hours ago.

I was still in a bit of shock, and for the first while my mother held the baby. Then they took her off to clean her up and brought him back and I held her. She's beautiful now but she looked weird when she was born – with a lop-sided red little face. But she looked up at me and held onto my finger with her little hand and I felt an incredible mix of emotions. I still couldn't believe it but I had to get used to it.

In some funny ways I think it's the best way you could have a child. None of the worry and anticipation, just a sudden shock and there you go. Of course we were completely unprepared. Ruth and I had to go and stay with my mother while Leon sorted the flat out and got some baby things.

He'd gone from being stunned to being a proud little father in a day or so. His parents were the same as mine, angry to start with but then they couldn't stay angry too long once they saw little Ruthie for real. He got all the cot and clothes and painted up the spare room to make a nursery within a week and then there I was, a mother with my new baby.

I got used to it real fast. I always loved Ruth. We didn't have another one for the first few years because we had to get our finances straight, but she had a little sister three years ago and another one last year, so now Leon's the proud father of three beautiful girls, and he's always on about how the men will all be after them when they're older. He's real protective and proud.

I wouldn't recommend to anyone to go through what I did – I mean you couldn't do it on purpose! But for me it worked out fine. I wouldn't have thought I'd be a mother so young, but this way they'll be all grown up when I'm forty and I like the idea of getting to know them as adults before I'm too old.

Karena, 29
Kabul

I remember very clearly the day that the coalition forces arrived in Kabul, and the Taliban were finally driven out. Life under the Taliban was terrible. I had had to give up my work and stay home, my brothers were forced to grow beards. There was terrible suspicion and hatred every-where because of their ridiculous rules and because of the informers and troublemakers who worked with them. So many wasted years, and that on top of the years of war that had gone before. I had never known normal life, but even the strange life I had lived had been made more intolerable by the Taliban.

To start with no one was sure that they were actually gone. There were rumours that the foreign fighters were still there, or that the Taliban were just hiding. But I saw the procession of fighters and journalists coming into the town on the main road, with no one left to fight them. Then my brother came back from the shops and told me that it was true that the Taliban had left town, and I knew that finally we had been saved from those terrible people.

I ran out in to the street and started telling everyone that the Taliban were gone, that we could do whatever we wanted. There were already little groups of people laughing and dancing to music – they had rescued hidden tape recorders and radios from attics and were now behaving in a way that would have had them beaten by the Taliban.

My brother was cautious about shaving his beard as he wasn't sure that something might not go wrong. But there were men shaving out in the street as a show of defiance, and I saw many men with bare faces for the first time in years. It was a beautiful, beautiful day for my poor city which has suffered so much from fanaticism and lunacy. Since then, not everything has lived up to the joy of those first days. I have moved away to London to study. But I will remember those days all my life nonetheless.

I was so happy being out with my friends. Some had make-up and uncovered faces, and it made me cry with pleasure to see that. You see that was forbidden under the Taliban. Even flying kites was forbidden – can you imagine it? Such a simple pleasure. Who could ever think that it was immoral? They were fools and the best day in my country's history was the day they left.

Thom, 42
London

Last year I was sacked from a job I had held for nearly ten years. It was quite an upsetting experience.

They are quite a big corporate company, but one that is run in a fairly autocratic way by the owner, who is the major shareholder. I always had an uneasy personal relationship with him, but my line manager knew that I did a good job for the company. A lot of people there did come and go, but having survived for so long in a fairly cutthroat environment, I didn't feel particularly threatened.

After the quarterly board meeting, which I attended, the owner asked me to stay behind. He started to ask me a lot of quite brusque and aggressive questions about my department and why its results were slightly down. I answered these quite calmly, and tried to explain everything. But in the end I became quite irritated because a lot of the issues he was attacking me for were company-wide problems and ones for which I didn't have any personal responsibility. For instance he started talking about the design budget, for which I am not responsible, but when I pointed this out he just shouted something about me trying to pass the buck. It was all quite annoying, but I didn't think it had gone especially badly nonetheless.

A few days later I arrived at work and found that my computer wouldn't log me on. I thought it was an IT problem and called the engineers, but they seemed a bit guarded and only promised to come round "later." Then my line manager arrived and called me into his office. I had a fairly good personal relationship with him, but on this morning he was very formal and solemn.

He told me that a decision had been made to make my position redundant. I knew immediately that this wasn't the truth and that the owner had told him to get rid of me. Things like that happened all the time. And when I told my manager that it was clear that he knew, but it was impossible for him to tell the truth without endangering his own position. In a company like that you have to everything by the book. So they went through all the formal stuff about how I could look for an equivalent position in the company and whatever. But I knew and he knew that that was just going through the motions and that I was out.

To his credit, he did make sure I got a reasonable pay-off. It meant that I would be okay for six months or so. But at the time this was not much consolation. I went back to my desk, and picked up a few things. He had told me I could come back for my other possessions any time, so I left most of it there, just took my bag coat, and a few photos.

It felt very strange walking out the door. I had been there such a long time, and had managed to adapt myself to surviving in a tough company, but now suddenly all that was gone.

I was very angry, not at my manager who was just a

pawn, but at the owner. He had clearly sacked me in a fit of pique, as he so often did, without any real understanding of the contribution I made to the company. I had never liked him much but I had devoted a lot of time to his company, to making money for him and his colleagues. And now he was throwing me away just like that.

I also felt quite panicky. I have a mortgage, I have a wife and two daughters, and they depend on me. I support them and the idea that I might not be able to look after them properly was terrifying.

Finally behind all that, I felt oddly elated. Because all the tensions and worries I had that had built up about work were suddenly gone. I didn't have to care about the end of year report, or the quarterly assessments or pay rises or bonuses or anything like that any more. That is a very liberating feeling. I've left a few jobs in my life, and there is always something of a feeling of freedom, but in this case it was just a tremendous relief.

I knew that my wife had her sister visiting for the day, and I didn't want to ruin her visit by going home, so I decided to stay out for the day. I didn't have any real plans, so I went for a long walk towards the centre of town, across the waste ground behind Kings Cross, and down through Bloomsbury towards Oxford Street. I stopped at a library just to look up the rules about redundancy, and to see what my options were. I did have the option of taking it to a tribunal, but I would have had to prove that my position wasn't technically redundant, and that they had replaced me. I knew they were smart enough to avoid being caught out, and also that they had access to expensive lawyers. I decided that any kind of legal follow-up would just bog me down in worrying about them when the best thing to do was to forget all about it.

When I got to town I went to the swimming pool. I had my stuff as I had been planning to swim at lunchtime. It was now about 11.30 a.m. and the pool was just about empty. I had a long slow swim. To start with I was still very agitated, but as I swam I got calmer, and felt my body start to relax a bit more.

When the lunchtime crowd started to arrive, I left and went to a little Italian restaurant I know. I had a lovely cheap meal there, and then set off to walk back towards home. I walked because that way it would take long enough to get there at the usual time. I wandered in and out of a few shops on the way, and bought a couple of books at a second hand bookshop. I sat in the park to read for a while, but instead I just sat there and thought about what to do next.

The thing I realized was that while I had been working at that company I had gradually changed. I had accommodated myself to their way of doing things, which was quite harsh and unforgiving, and in the process I had become coarsened myself. There's a degree to which you have to become tougher and less idealistic as you get older. You have to learn how to look after your family after all. But working there had almost made me forget who I was.

I sat there with the book unopened next to me on the bench and watched squirrels running around looking for nuts. And I wondered what to do next. I thought hard about the person I had been before I had got involved in that job. I realized that I didn't have to go back in time and forget everything I had learned – but I did have an opportunity to take a step back and decide what sort of person I wanted to be now. I also had the opportunity to catch up with old friends and spend some time doing things I really enjoyed.

It's not that I wasn't still scared. Of course I was, and that would stay with me until I got another job or found another way to be financially stable. But I found myself focussing much more on the new possibilities in my life – possibilities that had been hidden by the work I had been doing.

Then, at about 5.30 p.m. I got off the bench and started to walk home to see my wife. I knew she would be as worried as me and I wasn't looking forward to telling her. I even considered stopping at the pub to have a drink or two first, but I quickly realized that I would be best off going straight back. One of my clearest memories of the day is standing at the front door with my key, taking a few moments to think before I went in because I was so concerned about how upset she would be. But actually she was surprisingly calm. It wasn't that she had expected it as such, but she always knew that that company wasn't the perfect place for me. If anything she took it better than me, even though we did have some difficult times as a result.

In the end it was a good thing for me that I lost that job. It did take me a few months to get any more work at all, and then it was six months after that before I found a job I actually wanted. But in the meantime I did find out a lot about myself, and I was able to spend time with my family that I would otherwise have missed. And the job I found in the end was much better suited to me – a much nicer company run by people I respect. I wouldn't want to have to go through it again, but I think it's quite valuable to have a day like that every five or ten years. A day when everything gets turned upside down so that you can take a step away and see things from a completely different angle. Even though I'm now doing the same kind of work I was doing before, I now feel like it is something I made a positive choice to do rather than something I am just trudging along doing for the sake of the money, so I feel better about myself. And the fact that my wife was so supportive through a difficult period makes me love and appreciate her all the more so in that way it has also been a blessing.

Ben, 40
London

I was caught up in the fire at Kings Cross when I was younger. About forty-five people died. I was lucky because I was nearly out of the station when things started to happen. There was a strong smell of smoke as I was going up the escalator, and I always wondered if I could have done more to help by warning people or telling the staff.

I didn't because you just get on with things and assume someone else is dealing with it. Probably it wouldn't have made any difference anyway because by the time I got to the area by the ticket office, people were suddenly running from behind me shouting about the fire. We just ran towards the exit and got out. Upstairs, I didn't know what to do. My heart was pounding, and everyone was milling around, not sure what to do. Some of the people

who got out were coughing and spluttering from the
smoke. There was a woman crying because she had lost
her friend so I tried to calm her down, and then luckily
she found her friend, who was also in a state looking for
her.

I got some water for a man who was coughing and by
then the emergency services were arriving and running
into the station. So I just left. I didn't realize at the time
how bad it was. Because so many people had run up
behind me, and because I hadn't seen the actual fire, I
thought that there had been a fire on the platform or
something and that everyone would probably get out.
When I got home there were loads of messages on the
answerphone asking if I was alright – a lot of people knew
I travelled that way.

I turned on the television and was shocked at what I
saw, at how many people had died in the fire. I realized
how lucky I was.

The immediate effect of this on me was that I felt
terribly guilty. I felt bad because I had been lucky and
others hadn't been. And I felt guilty because I became
convinced that I could have done more to help.

But over time I came to realize that blaming yourself or
suffering from guilt are common reactions to this kind of
terrible situation. Even people who weren't there had
some similar reactions. I still dream about it sometimes.
But I stopped blaming myself. And then I realized how
fragile life is and vowed to make an effort to live the best
life I could.

I quit my job and went travelling to see some of the
places I had always wanted to. And when I came back I
was much more motivated about finding the right job and

trying new experiences. I suppose I realized that you do only live once, so it's no good wasting this life when it could end any day.

Anna, 36
Adelaide

I left my husband on my thirty-third birthday. It was a painful and difficult decision. He hadn't really done anything to deserve it. We had been married ten years, and I had just come to feel that we had gone as far as we could together.

To start with everything had been fine in our marriage. We always had a great time together, going on holiday, going out together.

By our late twenties, we had slowed down a bit as we were saving for a house. We went out less and stayed in more. I started to find that we perhaps didn't have as much in common as I had once thought. Once you took away the crowd of people and the exciting things to do, we didn't talk as much about anything I wanted to talk about.

He seemed to spend more and more time on his Playstation or going out with his mates. I didn't mind as my work meant that I did a lot from home, and it was good to have some peace. But we got into a kind of rut where more and more he treated the house as though it was a hotel, and I was there just to look after him and to be there when he needed me to be – for sex or whatever. But it didn't feel to me like there was anything I needed from him any more.

Then in our early thirties we started talking about having children. And I convinced myself that everything was fine, and that we were just going through the thing that all couples must go through, of growing older and more comfortable with each other.

I wasn't totally sure I wanted children, but I didn't want to wait until I was too old and miss the chance. And I had been with Andy for the best part of a decade, so surely this must be the right relationship for me to have a child in?

A few things happened after that. Firstly I developed a terrible crush on a guy called Brett who I worked with. I had been working with him for a while and had always found him attractive. But suddenly I started getting goose-bumps and blushing whenever he was around, and flirting with him every chance I got.

I thought about him all the time, and when I was with Andy I would be thinking about Brett, imagining scenarios in which I ended up with him instead. I would fantasize about running away on holiday with him, or just about having an affair with him.

Maybe some people have this experience often in their lives, but for me to even think about another man was very unusual. I have a very faithful mentality and would never actually cheat on a partner. But here I was thinking about it all the time, probably for the first time in my life.

Around the same time I had a pregnancy scare. I was very late with my period, and the test I took was kind of ambiguous – neither really positive nor negative. That made me think that I must be pregnant.

I told Andy and he was delighted. And I tried to be delighted too. Maybe I even fooled myself that I was delighted. But the truth showed through the next week when my period started and I realized it had been a false alarm.

Andy was disappointed, but reassured me that it would happen eventually. But I was just hugely relieved. I realized that it wasn't about the baby. I still quite wanted to have one. But I really didn't want Andy to be the father. I couldn't see myself with him for the next twenty years while we looked after children together. Trying to picture that made me realise that I was mentally cutting my ties with Andy.

But I still couldn't just leave him. It was a terrible period for me, because I felt so guilty about the way I felt. But there was nothing I could do to change it.

Brett started going out with one of my friends (they're actually married now, with a new baby). I was a bit jealous, but I knew it wasn't really all about him. My crush on him had partly been a fascination with the idea that my life didn't have to be like this. And the fact that he wasn't available made no difference to how I felt.

On the day before my birthday, Andy told me he had been too busy to get the present he was looking for, and asked if he could take me shopping so that I could choose something for myself. It was typical that he had been too disorganized to get something, but I wasn't too bothered as I hadn't wanted to be beholden to him anyway.

On the day of my birthday, I told him I was feeling ill, and I just stayed in bed. Later in the afternoon I suggested that he go out with his mates. I said we'd postpone my birthday to another day since I was ill. Once he was gone, I packed my bags and wrote him a note. It was a few pages long, but that is the part of all this that makes me feel the most guilty. I should have been brave enough to sit down face to face with him and tell him I was going.

When I was ready to go, I packed the bags into my car (we each had one). Then I went back in and sat at the kitchen table for quite a long time, just staring around me. I was in a daze. I had half wanted to go for a while, but something had just snapped. It wasn't the present, although Andy probably thinks to this day that I left because he didn't buy me a gift.

It was more the fact that I had known that my birthday would be a bit of a trial, and that I was so relieved when I didn't have to do anything special with him. That was the last straw in terms of fooling myself I could still live with him. I had to go, and the sooner the better. But I still should have told him to his face.

In any case, after I had sat there for a while I just suddenly got up and walked out to the car, scared that I might change my mind. I was shaking so much I could hardly drive. I had to stop a few blocks away just to gather my nerves.

Andy's never forgiven me, and nor have a few of our friends. Some of them were truly spiteful about it. But sometimes in life you just have to accept that you are living a lie. And if you are doing that, it becomes impossible to go on the same way for even a day longer.

Hugo, 48
Birmingham

I lost a lot of money in the dotcom crash. It was my own stupid fault. I had been watching other people make lots of money from stocks and share options, and I had been jealous that everyone seemed to be getting richer than me. I wasn't that badly off, but I got my mind full of dreams about expensive cars and holidays in the Caribbean. It all seemed so easy because the stocks only ever seemed to go up.

Now of course I know that stocks can go down as well as up. But it seemed very different at that stage. Everything to do with the new economy seemed to be completely different. It was a mania really. People were buying and selling shares with no idea of how the companies involved could ever make money. The internet just seemed like this magical thing that no one could lose money investing in.

Also, I now understand that the point at which everyone in the world thinks you can't lose on something is the point at which the bubble is about to burst. In other words, by the time someone like me hears about an investment it is probably already too late. The smart money is already on the way out.

The point at which I joined in, some of the stocks were even staring to slump. I bought a few new issues, following my broker's recommendations, and tips from friends and newspapers. And they just went up and up. On paper I had made a big profit, with no real effort. I started to imagine I could quit my day job and just live off stocks and shares. A foolish idea!

Then a few of the stocks I had missed the boat on the first time, came down by about twenty per cent. Instead of realizing this was a slump, I thought I was being smart and buying bargains. I became obsessed with it and sank more and more of my money into it.

Then they just kept falling. And the stocks I had started with began falling too. There was a miserable slow grind down and down, and all the money I had made, and most of what I had invested, was wiped out over a two-year period.

The real nadir was when my house was repossessed. I had been unable to keep up mortgage payments because I had lost so much money that my salary was all taken up with paying off debts. It was absolutely horrible. I had to move back into a bedsit and try to start saving up to rebuild my life. Other people lost money too, but having bought at the peak, I got caught very badly.

Since then I have read a lot about mass hysteria and bubbles in history, and I realize that I got caught up in something that happens in all kinds of societies over time. It's a kind of delusion, powered by greed. In Holland they even had the Tulip Mania where people started paying the price of a house for tulip bulbs, only to have it all go horribly wrong in the end.

These days I have managed to rebuild my life. I avoided going bankrupt by the skin of my teeth, and worked hard to get straight over the last few years. I realized there's no magic get-rich quick formula I do actually hold a few shares now, but only in small quantities, and nothing that could create a problem. They make a little money to add to my salary.

But I look round now and read about people throwing

money into property investment schemes or whatever the latest mania is, and I worry for them. I wish people would find out more about past bubbles and manias because it would help them to avoid making the same mistakes I made.

Jim, 54
England

I grew up in a poor part of West London. My parents moved to Spain, but I stayed in London because I liked it there. I trained as a plumber, and was doing fine. I had my own flat and was out with the lads most nights, down at the football at the weekend – a normal life like so many people around me.

When I was twenty-seven I was in a pub a couple of miles from my home, when a man got stabbed. Three blokes walked in, and just went straight up to him and stabbed him, then ran out. He was bleeding very heavily, and it looked like he was dying. No one went after them or anything.

Most people just ran away or got out as soon as they could. I tried to help the man. It was just me and the landlady trying to help – we managed to slow the bleeding down and kept talking to him while we waited for the ambulance. No one else lifted a finger. There were some girls screaming, but they weren't much use.

The ambulance and the police arrived at the same time. I told them everything I had seen and they took my details as a witness. A few other people had stayed outside so they had a few names as witnesses.

The man died that night in hospital. It was part of some

kind of gangland feud apparently. They knew who had done it. The real problem was that when it came to it, no one would identify the men who had done it except for me. Maybe some of them hadn't seen their faces, but mostly they were scared of getting involved. The police told me that the case depended on me, but to be fair they also warned that I might be in danger.

The trial was months later, and nothing happened. But the week before it seems that someone on the inside leaked my name. I had a visit from two hard men who threatened me and told me that if I testified they would kill me.

I went to the police to ask for protection, and when I got back that night my flat had been attacked – they had just gone in and trashed it, but not stolen anything.

I was pretty scared. The police weren't much use. They said I could go on some kind of witness protection scheme but it would take time to organize. They advised me to stay "somewhere safe," but couldn't suggest anything.

I was on my own basically, and it was terrifying. The only thing I could think of was to get in my car and get the hell out of London. I went to stay with my cousin who lives in Cardiff. It was a long drive to get there and he wasn't that pleased to see me as he only had a little place, but he put me up when I explained the situation.

Luckily I don't have family left in London because if I did they would probably have gone after them too. It's horrible that just for doing what you think is the right thing you can end up being hounded. It made me see society differently. It's like there a veneer of respectability over everything, but just under that there is a world that operates on brute force, threats and violence. And corruption too, because how else did they get my name, except through the police or the courts?

I wasn't sure what to do. I was scared for my life, and not sure I wanted to testify at all. I stayed in touch with the police, but I called them, and wouldn't give them my address or number. I couldn't be sure it wasn't them. I'd already decided that their witness protection might not be as secure as it's cracked up to be.

In the end I decided to do the right thing. The trial was awful. I had to stand in court and look into the faces of the three killers, who were all nasty pieces of work, and identify them. I was threatened in the toilets by someone from their family, and told that they were going to hunt me down and kill me.

The police did at least give me an escort out and took me to where I wanted them to, which was to a service station on the motorway, where I met up with my cousin. He took me back to Cardiff, but I didn't even want to stay with him, just in case. So I ended up travelling around for a while, until I settled down in a small town in the English countryside.

For a long time I missed London really badly. But I knew I couldn't go back and feel safe. And I saw the streets of the city as a dangerous place where thugs like the ones who threatened me ran everything. Maybe that's a bit over the top, but that was my perception at the time.

So I built myself a new life, from scratch. People here know me under a different name and don't know why I moved away. Fortunately you can be a plumber anywhere, so I settled in well enough. After a while I made new friends and started to enjoy life here. It's quite bucolic and calm, but in a nice way.

I go to see my parents now and then, but I just cut myself off from everyone other than that. I didn't want to put anyone into a risky situation. It's a long time ago, so now it probably would all be safe, but I have a different life now in any case.

Anton, 39
Berlin

I was there when the Berlin wall came down. I lived in East Berlin before that and even though life had changed a lot since I was a child, it was still a very strange society. Towards the end it seemed obvious that something had to give, but everyone knew what had happened in Czechoslovakia and Hungary in the decades before. It still seemed possible, in spite of *glasnost*, that the communist regime would survive.

Then there was that week of political meetings, wild rumours and strange parties that led up to the wall coming down. The city was getting out of control, and the soldiers and police didn't want to provoke any incidents. It was a wonderful time for us young people, but still tinged with real fear.

The day it all happened I was actually at home in bed with a cold. I had been at an all night party and had woken up in the morning with a fever. But I got two phone calls – one from a friend who had heard what had happened, and one from my aunt who wanted to check that I was safely at home. She thought it was a terribly dangerous situation and that I shouldn't get involved.

But I was young and it was a historic moment – I had to

go down to the wall. It was a weird scene by the time I got there. There were people up on both sides of the "no mans land" chipping away at the walls from both sides. There was loud rave music coming from a sound system on the other side, and on the East side there were all sorts of little tape recorders and people dancing with impromptu bands and performances. I saw people going past with bags of chippings from the wall, even with wheelbarrows. Everyone was laughing, even though there were armed police and soldiers everywhere. It seemed clear that they had been told not to intervene. They were even laughing and singing along.

In the space of a few days, everything had changed. Even the day before I wouldn't have believed everything could happen so simply. We had all been a bit scared, thinking that people might get killed or arrested, and that it would be a struggle. But in the end it was a massive party. After an hour or so I met up with a few people I knew – not close friends, but people I knew from around town. I had a few beers from a bucket someone had brought. I had completely forgotten about my cold by now.

I walked out into the gap between the walls at one point. There were a group of us from East Berlin, and coming towards was a group of young people from West Berlin. It was absolutely extraordinary – unthinkable. A girl walking towards me opened her arms and we gave each other a big hug.

Of course we had met plenty of West Berliners before, but in a completely different context. In this situation we weren't two individuals, but representatives of two halves of a culture that had been kept apart. Now at last we were truly back together.

No matter what else happens in my life there will probably never be a day as emotionally affecting as that one. It was a great moment of history, and I was there to see it.

Anna, 33
Florida

I spent some time in jail when I was twenty. It was so ridiculous. I was in a crowded bus coming home from work and had to push my way past this guy to get out. He had a big rucksack on, and seemed to be getting in my way almost deliberately. Then as I left he pushed me – it was weird.

As soon as I got out of the bus I realized that my purse wasn't in my bag. It was full of coins so it was quite heavy, and my bag felt too light.

Immediately I realized what had happened. I jumped straight back on the bus before the doors closed and started shouting at the guy. I knew it was him. I know that when people pick your pockets, they often give you a push at the same time to distract you from the feeling of them taking stuff from you. And he looked nervous as soon as I got back on.

I confronted him and started shouting at him to give me bag back. He just started shouting at me saying I was crazy. I asked people to help me and shouted at the driver to close the door, but no one would do a damn thing. The driver just left the door open. It was incredible. I had caught this guy, and he was right there, but no one would help me get my purse back. What are people like?

The guy tried to push past me and I pushed him back quite violently. I can look after myself. I look quite small but I go to the gym and work out and I am strong. You don't want to mess with me. Besides which, he was not that big, and he was old, about forty.

Eventually he just shoved his way past me and started running. Even when it was so obvious that he was robbing me, still no one did anything. I jumped off and chased after him.

He ran down a side street, with me behind him. I chased him for about a minute, but he was getting away from me. Then as he was running across a street he almost hit a car and I made up the ground. I came up behind and tripped him and he fell to the ground.

By now I was absolutely furious. I started kicking him hard, and kept kicking until I was sure he couldn't get up. In truth I probably was much too violent, but I was so angry in the heat of the moment.

Eventually I was done, and he was lying there, not unconscious, but quite badly beaten. I reached down and opened his jacket, and right there in his inside pocket was my purse. That was my biggest mistake. At that moment someone ran out of a house beside me and told me the police had been called.

I actually stood there waiting because I was in a bit of a daze and I thought that they were coming to take him away. It really didn't occur to me they were coming for me.

But that's what happened. I was arrested for assault and battery. He had the cheek to stand up in court and say that I had attacked him for no reason. No one had seen me take my purse back. I couldn't track down anyone who had been on the bus. As far as the law was concerned I had made an unprovoked attack on him. It's incredible, but I ended up in jail for a month. I had actually had some minor problems with the police in the past and that didn't help, but in this case it was completely unfair.

I won't tell you about my time in jail. It wasn't great but it wasn't the worst. I survived, that's all I can say. But when I came out I had lost my job, and my boyfriend had moved out and disappeared. I had to move back in with my family, and start from scratch. It was dreadful. My whole life felt like it had been pulled out from under my feet.

I had to start all over again, and work my way up from nothing. In one way it did me a favour though. I had been working for a low wage. Now I found it really hard to get a proper job, so I did whatever it took to get from where I was to a point where I could set up a business for myself. It took years of hard work, but I got to a point where I felt like my finances were under my own control again.

I have mixed feelings when I look back. It is something that defined my life. It was completely unfair, but in the end I learned a lot about myself

Looking back to the original situation, I don't know what I should have done to this day. I know I could have been less violent, but what else do you do in a situation like that? You have to protect yourself.

Marlon, 33
New York

I'm incredibly lucky. On 11 September 2001 I was scheduled to have a meeting in the World Trade Center. The weekend before I was building a wall in my garden. I managed to knock over a pile of bricks onto my foot and broke two toes. It was extremely painful. My girlfriend had to get me to the hospital, and they put me in plaster and gave me painkillers then sent me home.

There was no way I could get around that week so I cancelled all my meetings. I stayed home, watching television, reading the papers and getting on my girlfriend's nerves in the evenings by moaning about my foot.

On the morning of the 11th, she was still home having breakfast, and I was in bed half awake, when she came in and told me something was going on and I had to come and watch.

Just as I started watching, news came of the second plane. We just sat there on the floor holding onto each other. We're way up town, but we still felt like we ought to be going into a cellar somewhere or fleeing. But we couldn't move away from all those terrible images on the television. And then the towers started falling, right there in front of us. You couldn't see them from where we live, but they were something I was used to seeing on a daily basis and I simply couldn't believe what I was seeing. Me and millions of other people.

She knew that I was supposed to be at a meeting in the World Trade Center, and she just kept crying about it, and to be honest I did the same. We were scared and we knew the world was changing in front of us. But we also knew that I had had the luckiest escape of my life.

I felt guilty too. I might have survived – my meeting was a few floors down, but it was high enough that it would have been risky. I spent days afterwards scouring the papers and watching the TV news to try and work out what would have happened, but who can tell.

The man I was supposed to be meeting made it out – I didn't manage to talk to him on the 11th, but I got through to someone who had his mobile number at a different branch the next day and talked to him. He told me that people he knew had disappeared and that he was still waiting on the news. I fear for the worst, although I never did get to see him again. He left the company he worked for, and I never spoke to him after that.

I felt guilt because I saw people dying on the television and knew that it could have been me. There's no point in getting too tied up in knots about it because that is just the way things happen. I was lucky and I have to cope with it and get on with life.

If I had spent too much time obsessing about that I would only have been making myself a victim, where I was in fact the lucky one.

But it did make a huge difference to my life. I had the most intense feeling about everything in my life – all the good things seemed like a massive blessing, and anything bad seemed like the worst thing in the world. I had enormous mood swings all the time.

I found that in the morning when I got out of bed I would be literally blessing the world around me because it seemed so extraordinary that I still had all these things.

I asked my girlfriend to marry me a few weeks afterwards. I had always felt that we would marry some day, but suddenly it seemed like there was no reason to wait for anything. We had to live in the here and now. I understand that in wartime people have a tremendous sense of urgency about the details of everyday life.

My grandmother once told me that in the second world war she had the happiest times of her life, and the saddest times, and I think something similar happened to me after 9/11.

Realizations and Epiphanies

My editor has asked me to define "epiphany." It is an interesting word because it has a strong religious connotation, as it comes from a word that means a sense or manifestation of a divine being, Christ in particular.

However "epiphany" has come to be used to mean a sudden sense of understanding of the world, as though everything is in its rightful place, and one suddenly understands the world clearly – for the religious, this would involve an understanding of God's scheme for the world. For agnostics, the term is still relevant because one can have the same sensation of feeling that everything in the world makes sense and fits together in a euphoric way.

The accounts in this section include a number of cases in which the teller came to a new understanding of the world, and did so with a heightened sense of happiness that lent their new understanding a feeling of profundity. For instance Shelley, who came to understand a very different way of seeing the world while standing in the turquoise sea, came at the same time to a new understanding of what it is to be happy. Perhaps we often need to take a step back and consider how we understand happiness, and whether or not the things in our life which we define as good things are indeed sources of good and happiness.

For Dana and Ella, the experiences described here are epiphanies in the traditional sense, in that they are moments when they came to understand and perceive

Christ in a new way. For Karen the epiphany was much more of a political realization, when a new experience made her see her life and surroundings in a new way.

There are other accounts in this chapter where the teller has simply come to a new understanding of their life and the way they are living it. For Dan, Cinnamon and Terry this realization goes to the heart of their lives and their expectation of how they should live. For Terry it is an understanding that is brought to his life by an understanding teacher, whereas for Dan and Cinnamon it is a more personal understanding that they reach through the decisions they describe.

We assume that as we grow up we reach a "settled" stage of our life, where our beliefs and attitudes are set in stone. But this sometimes leads us to accept ossified attitudes and received ideas rather than challenging those attitudes constantly and questioning our own motives and ideas. The more we keep an open mind as we go along, the more chance we have of coming to new understandings of ourselves.

Anton, 34
Walsall, England

This probably only means something to me, but the day I qualified as a dentist was a day when my life completely changed. I had a job lined up to go to, but while I was a student I had been living a student lifestyle, and I had been working washing dishes in a local vegetarian restaurant.

It was hard work, and paid terribly. The hot water used to run out all the time, so we were stuck in a sweaty basement kitchen, going in and out of hot and cold water, washing pans that were caked in burnt cake mix, soup pans, all that kind of thing. At the end of a shift you would come out and smell like all the food – I used to have to go home and have a shower before I felt human.

All the time I was going between the restaurant and working hard for my exams, and it was a tremendously hard grind for me. I had often despaired of ever managing to get through it. I had to work so hard for enough money to survive, that I wondered how I could ever study.

Eventually I got to the end, and I qualified. The day I got the good news I was booked in to work the evening shift at the restaurant, but they knew I would probably leave. I thought about just not going, because it seemed like such a drag, but I knew I would be letting the people I worked with down if I did that. So I went in. It was actually a very quiet evening, but it seemed to last a long time. I was truly tired washing up at the back, but also very happy, because every time I washed a pan I could think, that's the last time I'm ever washing you.

When we finished we had to clean up as usual – it

used to take about half an hour after the last customer left. We did that with the music up loud, dancing around a bit as we cleaned. The two people I was working with were both good friends, and they were happy for me. They were both actors or musicians and worked there to get some money in between jobs, so for them it was a permanent way of life, but they had always known that I was working to move on to my professional job, and they were genuinely pleased for me. Then, at about half-past eleven, one of them, he was the shift manager, brought out a few champagne glasses, and opened a bottle of cheap cava, and we drank a toast. I was quite touched.

Then I got my stuff and left. I was going on a cheap holiday the day after then coming back to work, so I just went home to wash and go to sleep. But I remember how excited and optimistic I felt. It was like being on the boundary between two completely different lives, and it felt great.

I always try to remember what it was like to work in that restaurant. Now that I am wealthier I think it does me good to not be too arrogant about it and to remember how hard people work in those kinds of jobs. My wife sometimes tells me off because I tip too much and don't always complain about bad service, but I remember exactly what it's like and if I can be nice to them I will be.

Tom, 48
Derbyshire, UK

I lost my driving license for two years. It was my own fault of course. I'd picked up a few points on my license here and there over the years and then I got caught speeding, a long way over the limit.

To start with, I had absolutely no idea of how I was going to cope. I have been driving since I was seventeen, and I am completely used to doing everything with the car. I live two and a half miles from the train station and my workplace is a fair distance from the train station in town. I really thought I wouldn't be able to cope.

I bought a bicycle and tried it to get to and from the station. It turned out that I am allowed to take the bicycle on the train, so I was also able to ride into work at the other end, although sometimes I instead left it locked up at the station. The first time I got on the bicycle was very strange. They say you never forget how to ride a bike, but I hadn't even sat on one for twenty years or more, and it felt very precarious.

I managed to get going, a bit wobbly at first, but steadily improving my balance. The first few days of this I was absolutely exhausted. I was straining muscles I didn't even know I had.

I hated arriving to work all sweaty and tired, and having to change into different clothes. But as with all things you start to develop a routine. In the end I kept a set of clothes at the office to change into, and started to get used to changing.

At weekends I had to change my routines significantly. Shopping and going out were very different experiences. I

107

had to use the bicycle even at the weekends, although I did also take taxis for going out. I had sold my car, meaning to save money while it was out of action, so I didn't even own a car at this point. That saved me a hell of a lot of money every week, so that was a positive thing about the situation.

The good effects of this became apparent after a few weeks. I started to become much fitter because of all the cycling and walking. I had been feeling a bit old and slow, and wheezing in the mornings because I smoked. I had just put this down to getting middle-aged and ignored it, but now I realized that there was no need to feel that way. Everything about me started to feel better and more alert. My muscles were stronger, I lost weight and I even stopped smoking because the early morning cycle made me so conscious of how short of breath I was in the mornings, and that made even more difference.

I also realized how much you miss when you are in a car, shut away from the world. I don't know why I never noticed this when I was driving. But when you walk around a town you are much more part of the place, rather than just observing it through glass. You talk to people more, you see more of the detail. In short it is a much happier experience.

I'm just coming to the end of my ban so in theory I could start driving again, but I really think I might not bother. I have saved money, felt fitter and happier and changed my outlook on a lot of things in life. I'm worried that if I get the car again I might just slip back into old habits. Alternatively I might just get an old car for a weekend run-around – the shopping would be a lot easier with a car, I must admit. But I don't want to lose the gains I have made. It is strange how something quite problematic at the time turned into the best thing that could have happened to me.

Dana, 34
Scotland

I was brought up as a Catholic. I rebelled against it at an early age. I found all the ceremony ridiculous, and I found it hard to believe that, if there was a god, he really wanted us to go through all the rigmarole of masses with robes and incense and all that stuff. My grandfather was an atheist and spent a lot of time telling me what a lot of nonsense it all was.

As a result I had nothing to do with the church for many years. Then, two or three years ago, I was driving up to the far north when I passed a rickety old chapel up on the hills. I don't know what possessed me, but I went in and sat down at the back. It was a sweet little place, a bit rundown, but with a little altar and a few prayer books and Bibles on display. I have no idea what denomination it was, or who looked after it. There were a few cottages within sight of the chapel, but they were all pretty far away.

At the time I had been going through some difficult things. My marriage had broken down and I had changed career. I had also been having arguments with my mother which made life stressful. Mostly she was disappointed that I wasn't doing things the way she had, settling down with a house full of kids, being the proper family girl she always wanted me to be.

109

Anyway, whatever it was that made me go into the church, I started looking at the bible while I was there. I leafed through it, and every time I opened it at a page there seemed to be something that related to me, or that I thought was important about life in general. I realized that I had split from the church because of all the surface things, but that I had let that distract me from the underlying issues.

I sat at the back of the church with the bible closed on my lap, and I thought about my life. And I realized that the thing that was missing was God. Even though I had fallen away from him, there was something deep down in me that believed there was a real god. If anything I felt that the priests and choirboys I knew as a child were dishonouring Him.

I knew I couldn't go back into any normal organized church. I felt too strongly about the way that churches distort the teaching of Christ. But I finally realized that that was no reason for me not to live my life according to the Bible. I don't know why it took me so long to come to this realization, but there in that chapel I just felt the presence of God very strongly. I realized He had been there all along, even when I wasn't paying attention to Him.

Since then I have tried to live my life with Christ as far as I can. I have been to a few non-denominational prayer groups and discussion groups, because I feel that sometimes you have to share your experiences. But mostly I feel that my religion is something that is very private, and something that I need in my life, without needing to involve others in my worship.

Karen, 25
New Jersey

I grew up in a rich family, with a very protected view of the world. So far as I was concerned, all Americans had swimming pools and big houses and gardens, and life in America was a wealthy, comfortable one. Maybe I'm exaggerating slightly, but I had that truly sheltered mentality.

It wasn't my parents' fault. They were well to do, but they tried to educate us about the world. My mother was involved in a lot of charity work and she would try to get us interested in it, by telling us about it. But is all just seemed so boring.

I suppose what I am trying to say is that I was a brat. I'd been to New York a few times with my mother or aunt, but we just drove in and shopped and came away again.

My mother was involved in a literacy charity, and one day in the summer vacation she asked if I wanted to go into the city with her. She was going to look at one of the projects that the charity supported, but afterwards she was going into town, and we could get some coffee somewhere and look at the shops.

I agreed, thinking that the project would be boring, but that I could put up with it for an hour or so. It was in a rough part of the Bronx. I had driven through the boroughs on the way into town and had seen all the tenements and run-down buildings, but I'd never really thought about it. But now we parked in this desolate street. My mother seemed quite at ease, but I was scared of all the people who stared at us as we went by.

The project was a kind of playgroup, where parents

could leave their kids while they worked. I think there was a charge, but the charity made it cheap enough that people on low wages could afford to use it. It was mostly Black and Hispanic kids, with a few others here and there.

The building was nothing but a shack. It smelled weird, and I immediately regretted coming. My mother wasn't bothered at all, and was chatting to the people in charge as though she did this kind of thing all the time. I was scared, and a little repulsed by the poverty and strangeness of it all.

Then my mother told me that she had a few things to talk about, and the teacher asked if I would help with some of the kids in the meantime. I couldn't really say no. So I had to sit down on the ground with a group of little kids, and read them picture books, for a long time.

I did relax a bit once I started doing that because they were all so fascinated by the books. And the questions they asked about things were funny because they were so odd. It took me a minute to understand some of them because they had such strong accents, but I started having fun with them.

It seemed to go on for quite a while, before my mother finished with her business and came to get me. I told the kids I had to go, and three of them started hanging on to my legs and hugging me, begging me not to go. It was bizarre. They were so grateful just because I had sat and given them some attention. It made me start to think about how hard their lives must be compared to mine.

My mother asked if I minded staying just a bit longer, so I did, and we played some games and read some more books. By the time I left there were four or five little kids all hugging me good bye and asking when I was coming back. Back in the car my mother thanked me for being so patient with them and explained that a lot of them didn't get close attention at school, so they really appreciated it when they went to the group.

We went into town and went to the shops, and for the first time I saw the contrast between the shiny wealth of Fifth Avenue and Broadway and the poverty we had just seen. It makes the city look completely different when you perceive the contrast.

We went back to the group a few times that summer. I actually asked my mother to take me again. I started to enjoy it, although it also broke my heart sometimes because you would build a real connection with some little kid just for an hour or so, but then you had to go back to your world and he had to go back to his. I'm not kidding myself I made any difference to anyone. But I think my mother knew what she was doing when she took me there. For the first time I understood the extremes that exist in this country and that we need to all look for each other in one way or another.

Maybe it's a bit like the shock that a lot of people got after New Orleans flooded – to see all those poor people and the gap that existed is truly shocking. But it is also a spur to action, because there are things you can do to make things better, and to help other people help themselves. I've always tried to remember that in the way I live my life.

Shelley, 29
Lesbos

I used to get quite depressed. I was living in Belgium and doing a well-paid, high-pressure job. I thought I was doing well in life. I spent a lot of time keeping up with the latest cultural trends and trying to know all the right people, brands and places to go. I would go to the trendiest new restaurant as soon as I heard about it. And when I went away with friends or boyfriends I used to go on city breaks, to cultural cities with museums and lots of good shops. And in spite of everything I often had very black moods. I would retreat into myself and not want to speak to anyone. I didn't know what was wrong.

Then two years ago I started going out with a very nice boy called Marc, who worked as a computer programmer. We wanted a holiday and he suggested a beach holiday in Greece. I couldn't believe he wanted to just go to the beach and hang around. I'd never done that in my life. I always wanted to do things and go places, and I thought I'd be dreadfully bored.

We went to Athens and got a ferry down to an island called Naxos, a very beautiful mountainous island full of olive groves and lovely white beaches. We were staying in a little place about fifty yards from the beach. All Marc wanted to do was potter to the beach in the morning, have a bit of a swim and read a book. Then a bit of lunch, followed by much the same in the afternoon. The old town was a tiny place, but we went in to get food at one restaurant or another in the evening, and then we used to be so tired we would fall asleep early.

For about three days I was bored and restless. I kept

muttering about wanting to do something, but Marc just asked why, when the place we were was so lovely. He used to ask me why I always wanted to do something when I was so busy in my normal life, and tell me I needed to relax. Then for some reason, after about three days, I managed to slow down to his speed.

On the fourth day I got up before him, quite early in the morning. The sun was low in the sky, and I walked over to the beach and across the dunes in my flip-flops. I walked down to the sea and just walked out in the sea about ten yards, so that the waves were lapping about my feet.

Even at seven in the morning the sun was getting hot. The sand was very white, and the water was an extraordinary turquoise. I stood still there and after a few minutes, all these little tiny fish started swimming around my feet. It tickled, but I was fascinated watching them.

While I was standing there I had this feeling that all my worries and anxieties were draining away from me, washing out into the sea somehow. I felt completely calm, for perhaps the first time in years. And I felt wildly happy.

I stood there for about an hour, not really thinking about anything, just enjoying being there. Then I went and bought some pastries and went back to wake Marc up. I didn't even tell him I'd been to the sea.

After that I had a wonderful holiday. I wasn't really in love with Marc, but we were great friends and once I stopped wanting to do things all the time we had a great time. We even went to see a few ancient stones and chapels one day when it was cloudy, but in a very lazy way. It wasn't something to tell people at home about, or to take pictures of, just some very interesting ancient relics, and a picnic up on the mountain.

115

When we got back to Brussels after two weeks away, I found my life peculiar. I couldn't get back up to the speed of city life, and I wasn't sure I wanted to. I started to get depressed again, and to worry. But every time that happened, I thought about that image of me standing in the sea with all the fish swimming around my feet.

I realized that a lot of things I had been obsessed with were just about fashion and keeping up with other people, and I wasn't sure I wanted to do that any more. I know everyone comes back from beach holidays with romantic notions. And the Greek Islands are notoriously romantic and fascinating, because they are so beautiful and relaxing at the same time as being ancient cradles of civilization. But I think this was a bit more than a romantic notion. The holiday just made me realize that there was another way of seeing the world.

I started planning an escape, and saving my money instead of spending it on keeping up an image. I wasn't seeing Marc any more, though we stayed good friends.

By the following spring I had enough and I set off to travel around the Mediterranean and the Aegean. I saw a lot of places through that summer, and at the end of it I decided to stay on. I rented a cheap room in Lesbos over the winter – quite easy to do once all the tourists go away.

The winter was fascinating. Colder than you'd think and quite bleak, but also very inspiring and charming. Then this spring I got a job in a bar at the beach, and I'm still here. So after a year and a half of this completely different life as a drifter, I am still loving it. I don't know who the latest bands are, what brands are trendy, what exhibitions have been on or anything like that, and I really don't care. Maybe some time I will go back to a more "normal" life, but if I ever do I will have a completely different attitude.

Ella, 39
San Diego

I found Jesus when I was twenty. I was brought up as an atheist – my parents were very much part of the sixties generation and believed in humanism, or in other words love and peace. And that's how I was brought up. There's nothing wrong with it, but I suppose I always felt that there was a kind of gap behind the whole idea of why we should be good to each other.

I had vague notions of Jesus and the Bible, but they were quite strange remote things to me in my childhood, and not something I ever knew something about.

Things changed one day when I was on a long drive through the desert. It was a baking hot day and I was driving along with the top down on my car, with a couple of hundred miles to go in my journey.

I had been listening to music on the radio, but I became restless, and looked around for something different. I got to one of those preacher stations you find everywhere. I wouldn't have stopped but the first thing on was a really lovely spiritual hymn. I listened to it simply because it was so nice, and then I didn't bother to change again when the man started preaching.

He wasn't one of these hellfire preachers, or someone just trying to get money out of me. Instead he was quite a calm reasonable speaker. And what he was talking about was why we should be good.

Two of the examples he came up with, neither of which I had come across before, were from Jesus' preaching. The first was the golden rule – "Do unto others as you would have done unto you." Once he explained a bit about the context in which Jesus was preaching, I started to understand that this was quite a profound piece of advice, and pretty much the basic point from which all morality develops.

Then he went on to the part where the Pharisees try to catch Jesus out by getting him to say that the Jews shouldn't pay their taxes to the Roman occupiers. Jesus wrong-footed them by showing them the picture on the coin, of Caesar, and saying that you should pay (render) unto Caesar what is Caesar's, and pay unto God what is God's. The preacher kept going round all the ways you could interpret this statement.

I was listening pretty closely by now, and I got really interested in the story. The first thing is the simple wisdom of sidestepping a question that was designed to embarrass him, with a smart answer. But beyond that there is something deeply wise about the whole idea.

There are things in the world that are of the world, and things of the spirit that are separate. One of the problems of my parents' generation is that they denied the spiritual side of humanity, or they tried to co-opt it either through sexuality and new-age ceremony, or through claiming that their ideals were spiritual ones. But they weren't. They were trying to mix up the problems of what you should pay to Caesar and what you should pay to God.

And when you start thinking about it that way, you also see how we can live fully in the modern world, fulfilling our responsibilities to society, using Jesus' golden rule, but at the same time we can consider what there is in each of us that is spiritual and separate to the worldly problems we face.

It seemed to me that in the space of two tiny statements, Jesus had solved the problems I had been dealing with my whole life – why should we be good, and how should we be good in the world?

After that there was another hymn, in praise of Jesus, and while I was driving along I felt a real warmth and light in me at the thought that Jesus was the person I should be following in my life. I can only describe it as feeling the holy spirit inside me at last, after years of denying that there was any such thing.

From that day onwards I vowed to educate myself with regard to Jesus and to become a follower of Christ. That has been the guiding principle of my life from that day to this.

Dan, 26
Washington

I was fifteen when I realized I was gay. I'd been having trouble fitting in around my friends when they talked about girls and dating. I always felt like I identified more with the girls than the boys, and I couldn't identify with the predatory, contemptuous way they talked about girls.

At the time I thought that this was because I had grown up with my mother and two sisters. I thought that it just

119

meant I had more sympathy with the female point of view.

But as well as being uncomfortable with the way boys talked about girls, I never met a girl I wanted to go out with. I used to get teased about it, but that's just how it was.

Then one day a new boy called Ivan arrived at school, in our grade. He was blonde and very athletic and as soon as I saw him a strange feeling came over me. He was a sports jock whereas most of my friends were more into music and books so we didn't make talk much. But whenever I saw him I couldn't take my eyes off him.

Even then it took me a week or two to realize what was going on. I thought I had a strange fixation on him because he was new and very different to me. Then late one night I was lying in bed and thinking about him yet again and it suddenly dawned on me that this was what it felt like to find someone attractive.

It was a strange moment because I felt ashamed and relieved at the same time. It was a small town and everyone around me had always despised homosexuality, and I had thought the same way. But at the same time it explained so much about the way my life had gone over the last few years.

I didn't do much about it for a while – I was just coming to terms with it gradually. I certainly never made a fool of myself talking to Ivan about it. He was a real jock and wouldn't have been at all amused.

Then I went away to college. I deliberately went to the city. And I was finally able to act on my attractions. I had a few short relationships, and then met Dave, my boyfriend, who I am still with.

The day I had realized I was gay was a weird day in my

life, but the hardest thing I ever did was to go home that first Christmas to tell my family that I was gay. I had talked to a lot of people about coming out of the closet. Some had told me not to, others had told me that they had done it and it was the best thing.

In the end I just didn't want to live a lie. My mother was always asking me if I had met a girl yet and assuring me that I would meet a nice girl in the end. I guess that she thought I was a bit backward and shy. In fact the opposite was true – I had felt very repressed at home as it is a small town, and I hadn't been able to meet anyone like me. But now I was absolutely fine and happy with my sexuality.

I got home on Christmas Eve and to start with I meant to tell them after Christmas was out of the way. But I was so nervous about it. I wasn't talking much and my mother kept going on and on at me because she was getting the idea that I was depressed. In the end there was no other choice.

I sat her and my sisters down and said I had something to tell them which might be difficult. Then I just came out with it.

My elder sister just laughed and said "I knew it, didn't I?" and then gave me a hug. My mother and my other sister were just sitting there looking a bit shocked. I could see my mother was a bit upset.

But then she did the bravest nicest thing she could which was to come and give me a hug too. She looked like she might cry, but she just said that whatever I did she would always love and support me.

My other sister ran out of the room and wouldn't talk to me all Christmas, so I guess I got every reaction I could have done.

After Christmas I went and told a few of my hometown friends too. I figured I had nothing to lose now. I didn't intend to go back and live there, but I thought people might as well know the truth.

We didn't talk about it at home much over Christmas. It was quite a strange atmosphere. Then the day I left my mother sat me down and we had a long talk about everything, and about how I knew and how long I had known, and was I being careful (of course). I could she was struggling to adapt but she really wanted to be normal about it. I was pleased.

My elder sister drove me to the station and told me that she'd always thought I was gay and had had a joke about it with her friends, but she was pleased for me if I was really doing what I wanted. She was the easiest one to talk to about it.

My little sister didn't really come round until she left school the next summer. I think she was worried about getting abuse at school for it, though that never happened. Anyway, in the summer she came to visit me in Washington. She seemed suddenly much more grown up, and she apologized for having been difficult about it. I told her it was fine – I had thought that everyone might be like that so I really understood.

The Christmas I came out of the closet was a very difficult one for me, but it was absolutely necessary. Until then I had had a furtive, secretive feeling because I was hiding my true self from my family and friends. Once I finally came out to them I felt completely liberated and able to deal with talking to anyone about it. After all if they could cope with it and if I could deal with them knowing then any other challenge looked a little bit easier.

Cinnamon, 44
London

This is a long story, and it doesn't all show me in the best light. I got married at thirty to my husband David. I had a good job in the media industry, and he worked in the city. For a few years everything was fine. We both worked hard, and earned good money. We had nice holidays and we could afford to go out and do whatever we wanted and also we could shop and indulge ourselves if we wanted to.

As I got towards my mid-thirties I started to worry about having children. I'm not sure that I had ever really thought that hard about it before then. It just started to feel like a lot of my friends were having children, and I started to think about the fact that I was going to end up being left behind.

We started to talk about it. And to discuss where we would live and how we would deal with it. Would we get a nanny and so on. We lived in an apartment in a busy part of town – lots of restaurants and bars but not many children's playgrounds. We started thinking that maybe we would have to move out of town and buy a house where the schools were good.

And we started trying for a child. I thought it would take a while. I had been on the pill for years and I had heard it can take a while after that to conceive. But to my surprise it happened right away. About two months after we started having these conversations, I was pregnant.

My friends with children were all very excited for me. My mother was over the moon. She had thought I wasn't going to get married in the first place, and then she had worried that I wasn't going to give her any more grand-children (she dotes on my little brother's three children).

I didn't really like being pregnant. I felt bloated and sick. I felt like my body was out of control and that there was nothing I could do about it. If I mentioned this to doctors or midwives they just nodded in a condescending way. I was used to people treating me with respect and now I had become some kind of breeding cow, for everyone to prod and examine.

But still I was looking forward to being a mother. Or I was sort of looking forward to it. I convinced myself that I was excited. Everything we had been speaking about as a notional idea seemed very real now. I had a picture of us living in the suburbs near a nice school. And me working part time or not at all, dealing with the nanny and talking to other mothers in the neighbourhood.

But at the same time there were other thoughts creeping through. I felt panicky at the idea that we were going to leave our lovely free life behind. I worried that my husband would leave me. I worried that I couldn't cope with a child. And above all I worried that when I saw other people's children, I still reacted with revulsion. Maybe that's putting it a bit too strongly, but I felt like the whole thing of clearing up a child's vomit or mess after a meal, and trying to keep the little things under control in a public place when they are having a tantrum and everyone is staring at you like you are a useless mother? I just felt like all that was beyond me, or nothing to do with me.

But I suppressed all those thoughts. I was going to be a mother. I did everything right. I looked after myself. We started to think about looking for a house we could buy.

Then one night in October, I started to feel quite ill. I kept having to get up in the night to be sick. And I had a terrible fever. I was about two and a half months pregnant. Not that far gone really.

I lost the baby. It was a miserable experience. Painful, difficult, emotionally draining. I was numb for a few days afterwards. I didn't really know what I thought.

Then I started to feel physically better and to reflect on the situation. I found I had two completely conflicting responses. I was genuinely sad about the baby. It was not very developed, but that was a tiny person who might have become my child. It is a very sad thing to go through.

But at the same time I had completely different response. Relief. Absolute, relief that I hadn't had to go through with it. I felt like I had been completely fooling myself that I wanted to be a mother. I felt that I had been reprieved from having to go through the motions of a life I no longer had to live. I didn't have to live my lovely life and my job, and the bit of town I lived in behind for some life of suburban, housewife drudgery.

The scary thing at this point was trying to work out what to do next. I was quite simply terrified of sharing how I felt with my husband. He had been so supportive through the whole pregnancy and through the miscarriage. I loved him more than ever. But all we had talked about for months was how we were going to be mummy and daddy to a little baby. How could I tell him I had changed my mind.

Eventually one night I plucked up the courage. It took a couple of drinks to be brave enough (I was allowed to drink again now I had lost the baby).

I broached the subject so carefully that it took him a

while to understand what I was really saying. Which was that the only way I could see my future now was not to have children. I didn't want children anymore.

When he understood, he went into another room for a while. I was desolate because I thought he hated me. But he came back and told me that he had the same problem as me.

He said that he was completely conflicted as well. Some days he could see himself getting on the morning train, coming home and reading books to the children. But other days he felt like that just wasn't him. And he also said he wasn't sure it was me either.

He said that if I ever changed my mind he'd be right there with me, but if I was sure I wanted not to have children, he'd be there with me too. It was the most important thing in the world to hear that. I'll always love him anyway, but that moment moved us on because it broke the last barriers between us. We can always tell each other absolutely anything, no matter how difficult.

It's actually quite difficult to be the only one without children in a group of friends. People act as though you're slightly disadvantaged. And you can't go on about all the good things in your life – the fact that your life and house are still your own, the fact that you are not someone's slave, and so on. Parents would be offended if you said things like that. And even worse they would give you pitying looks and shrug as though you are in denial about what you really want.

But I know that I found out what I really want from life. I want to be happy with my husband, and I want to go on living the life that we enjoy. If that makes me selfish, I'm sorry. But at least I found out that that was what I wanted without ending up trapped in a family life that I didn't want. In that respect, no matter how sad or jarring my story might be, at least I know for sure that I have made the right decision for me.

Terry, 24
Liverpool

When I was young, I thought I was stupid. I couldn't keep up at school at all. My reading and writing were way behind by the time I was eight, and all the work just made my head hurt. I was terrible at maths too.

The only thing I could do was draw. I was good at all arts things like painting and making things. I was the youngest of four children and everyone just assumed I was a bit dim but artistic. I think they were assuming that the best I'd ever do would be to go to art college.

When I was eight our teacher (I can't remember her name) went off to have a baby so we got a temporary teacher called Mr Barnes. I didn't like him at first because he was very strict and never seemed to smile. But he was fair, and only told people off if they deserved it. I started to get used to him.

From the start he was concerned about my progress. Where the previous teacher had just assumed I was stupid with everyone else, he came and spent a lot of time talking to me about things, so that even when my written work was terrible he made sure I was listening and understanding. As a result I started to feel more like I was part of the class, though my work was still no good.

After a few weeks I came in one day and he had

arranged for me to have some tests. I had to go out of the classroom and do a series of test with someone I'd never seen before. It was quite worrying because I thought that they were going to put me in the special class or send me away or something.

A few days later my mother got a letter asking her to come in with me one day. Of course she thought I was in trouble and put on her best clothes and came with me, telling me all the way what trouble I'd be in if there was something wrong.

But when we got there she spoke to the headmaster for a while, and then I had to go in with Mr Barnes. The tests he had organized had been for dyslexia. I'd never heard of it, and I don't think my mum had much idea either. But he explained that it was like a kind of color blindness, except that what I had trouble perceiving was words, letters and symbols. But especially words. As he talked about it, it all made a lot sense to me. The way that words seemed to swim in front of me when I tried to understand them.

He explained also that he thought I was a bright kid, but that I would need a lot of help and understanding if I was to progress in spite of the dyslexia.

My mum was mortified. I think she felt like they were criticizing her for not noticing herself. But then the headmaster apologized himself, saying that he felt it was bad that they hadn't picked it up sooner, and praising Mr Barnes for having taken the effort to work the problem out.

It made a huge difference to me. Firstly I got extra help – the teachers from then on took into account the fact that my verbal skills were better than my written ones. And also I got extra one-to-one help with my writing and maths and so on. So even though I was never going to be brilliant at written skills, I started to be able to keep up enough. Especially now that I realized I wasn't stupid, because that gave me the motivation to work hard to overcome my problem.

I did quite well at school in the end. I always had to work twice as hard to make my writing good enough, but I started to find ways to cope. I did a lot better once we started to use computers more too – spellchecks are such a fantastic thing for people like me!

I got to college and now I have a degree and a decent job. I really think that if someone like Mr Barnes hadn't sat down with me and tried to work out why I was sensible to talk to but no good at writing, I would have been left on the scrap heap my whole life. So I have a great deal to thank that teacher for.

Danny, 34
Essex

My parents were entrepreneurs. They did all sorts of things for a living, and life as a child was never dull. One day we would have a garden full of garden gnomes, another day my dad would have a lorry full of trampolines to sell. Never a dull moment.

My dad always tried to bring me up to understand money and how to make it work for you. We had very strict rules on pocket money and if we wanted something we had to save it for it and so on.

One day when I was ten we were out driving in my

dad's van. He'd picked me up after school, and then we had been to the supermarket. On the way back we passed a skip.

My dad stopped the van to have a look. It was obviously a house clearance as there was all sorts of stuff in there.

He told me to come quickly and help him to sort out a few things for the back of the van. There were some perfectly good bits of garden furniture, which he salvaged and ended up putting in our garden. He also got a big box of tools and nuts and bolts out of it.

Finally there was a box of toys. There was loads of things in there like Top Trumps (a card game), Yo-Yos, and bouncey balls. It was a bit of a treasure trove for me at that age. I asked him if I could keep them.

He told me that I could, so long as I shared them with my little sister. But then he said that if we were smart though, we'd just choose one or two things each, and then sell the rest to our friends at school.

It was an interesting idea, and after I talked to my sister about it, we had the idea of going a bit further and having a toy sale, with these and with some of our old toys which we were bored of.

We cleared it all with my mum and dad, and then invited a bunch of friends around on the Saturday. We laid out all the toys on tables, like a jumble sale, and had lemonade and cakes, so it was a bit of a party. The other kids were buying toys with their pocket money and then we were all playing out in the yard with everything. It was a good party.

But more importantly, when we counted the cash after everyone left, it came to about twenty week's worth of pocket money. We had done really well out of it.

It really planted the idea in my head of being an entrepreneur myself. It seemed so simple to take a basic idea, and a few things, and to sell them on at a profit. Of course, that is putting it too simply, but that day really set my mind racing. From then on I always had ideas about how I could make some money. I used to set up little lotteries at school, or get a tray of the latest toy wholesale, and sell them on. I tried all sorts of thing, and by the time I left school I was getting pretty good at it.

Since then I've never looked back. I've had a few good business ideas and some terrible ones. But the terrible ones just cost me a bit of pride, while the really good ones have done me proud, and now I have a pretty good living.

Death, Illness and Personal Tragedy

It is inevitable that death, bereavement and illness (death's shadow), will have a major impact on our lives. We start out living our lives as though we are immortal. Then at some point, usually in fairly early childhood, we come to understand that our time on the earth is limited.

We come to terms with this in various ways. We may turn for comfort to religion, or to humanistic concerns. We may decide on a positive outlook on life and death, or a nihilistic disregard for the possibilities that confront and worry us.

But in one way or another, we manage for the most part to put death and illness out of our minds, until we personally suffer from their effects. When a loved one dies, a common comment is that we couldn't imagine life without them. Our minds rebel at death, but we have to somehow cope with it nonetheless.

My heart aches when I read accounts such as those of Susan, Andy and Jana. No words will bring back their loved ones, and the sorrow they feel may never heal. Nor would they want the sorrow to fully heal, because that could only happen if they were to forget, and a crucial part of dealing with bereavement is knowing that you hold a place for the person who has died in your heart.

For many who have lost a loved one, the pain fades over time, but can return at the same intensity at any time, even years later, if something brings a sudden memory back from the past. One of the most difficult *things for those who suffered a bereavement is the general tendency to be supportive of their grief in the early days (when the loss hasn't fully sunk in) only to withdraw sympathy if the bereaved is seen to be suffering for a long time. People become embarrassed by extended grieving, but for some people extended grieving is the only option.*

Other accounts here deal with illness and suffering rather than with death. Illness always tends to remind us of the frailty of our bodies, and of the state of mortality in which we exist.

Any reminder of mortality tends to focus our minds on the lives we are living. When you consider the option that your life might end at any time, you tend to view your life in a different way.

Whether they recount lives touched by death or illness, all of these accounts demonstrate the powerful effect that such experiences can have in our lives.

Susan, 52
Seattle

My wonderful husband died on the tenth of July last year. He had a very aggressive cancer that affected his blood. From becoming ill to being diagnosed to the day he died it was only a few months. We really had no chance to prepare ourselves or to come to terms with what was happening.

I had been with him since we were at college together. We were very close, as friends as well as partners. He was the only person who knew everything there is to know about me, and he was the person I could always trust in any situation. I'm lost without him.

It even shook my faith because I found it hard to believe that God could let that happen. I pray all the time now, more than anything, that the pain for me might get easier to bear. I don't know what will become of me because even a year later I find every day a trial, while I used to be such a happy person. I didn't know how lucky we were.

I miss him so much, and I take consolation that we will be together again when I die. I love him as much now as I ever did.

Tom, 35
Yorkshire

I was in hospital once, because I had got in a fight after the pub closed. I got quite badly beaten up by a few men, and I had to stay in hospital overnight in case I had concussion. To be honest it had happened a few times to me. I was always getting drunk and starting fights. I used to say obnoxious things to people deliberately. It was almost like a Friday night wasn't complete without a bit of a fight to finish it off.

While I was in Accident and Emergency, when I first got there, another man of about my age came in, with a friend. He looked very pale, and as soon as he got there he had to lie down on the floor. It was very crowded and there didn't seem to be anyone to deal with him. All around there were people like me, lads who had got into fights. But his man was different. His friend told me that he had Hodgkins Disease, which I hadn't heard of then. He had fainted earlier in the day and they had tried to persuade him to come in, but he had wanted to avoid coming in because he was scared of what they might tell him. But then he had fainted again and they had panicked and brought him in anyway. Now they had to wait in A&E with all the people who'd been in Friday night fights, and drunk people shouting everywhere. I was a bit drunk myself, but I was coherent. I think getting punched in the head had sobered me up a bit!

While his friend was telling me all this, he seemed to be almost unconscious. Even though I was bleeding from a cut in my head, I went to try and get a nurse to come quickly. I was getting quite het up about it – it seemed wrong that he should have to wait with all of us, when for people like me it was our own stupid fault we were there. The nurses were very patient with me and promised to do their best.

When I got back the man had woken up properly – Dave was his name, and he talked to me while we all waited. He was very open about his illnes, and told me about some of the things he had gone through. It sounded terrible. As soon as he got one symptom under control he would hope that he was stabilizing and then something else would go wrong.

Eventually they came for him with a trolley, and I said goodbye to him – they took him away, then soon after that they came to stitch me up. They made me stay there in case I had any delayed concussion symptoms. I wanted to go home because I felt stupid taking up a bed, but they made me stay.

I stayed awake thinking about Dave. For some reason it made me realize how ridiculous it was that I was out endangering my health, drinking to excess and getting into fights, while here was someone who was suffering terrible illness through no fault of his own. I'd sometimes vowed to give up drinking before, and then of course it never lasted. But this was different. I realized what an idiot I had been, and truly felt like I had to change.

It didn't stop me going out drinking at the weekend. But finally I learnt to stop when I'd had enough, and I never got myself into fights after that. You could say that I finally grew up a bit. I don't know what happened to Dave. I think about him now and then, and I'm afraid he may have died. He was so ill it is hard to believe he could fully recover. But on the other hand medical science is getting better all the time, so who knows? I hope he did make it.

Andy, 38
Brisbane

My girlfriend killed herself a few years ago. It's hard to write about it. She was always a depressive, and as long as I'd known her she was on one medication or another, just so that she could sleep and cope with everyday life. I had known all this about her when we met. I'm quite an optimistic upbeat person, and I used to try and help her through the black times. If I was depressive myself I maybe would have found it harder to cope with her depressions.

She always used to tell me that she would end it all some day. She felt that nothing would ever go right for her. And of course if you are very depressed it tends to make it harder to progress and get anywhere.

We would argue sometimes about it. I guess I got frustrated that she never seemed to get better. But we were happy together in our own way. Maybe it was a bit strange at times, but you shouldn't have the idea that I didn't like being with her. I loved her and we had some great times. The difference always was that when she got depressed she couldn't remember the good times. Or she would say that they hadn't been so good after all, whereas I always remember them with happiness, and perhaps I managed to forget the bad times more easily than her as well. It's just a different way of seeing the world.

Also, a lot of what she went through was because of some bad things that happened to her as a child. I won't tell you all of that stuff, but if you knew what she had been through it was totally understandable that she should be down sometimes. In a way I felt guilty because my life wasn't so bad, and I felt I had to try to look after her.

When she did it, it came out of the blue. I knew she had been having a bad week or two, but I didn't think things were so bad. She didn't leave a note or anything. She'd always said she wouldn't and that I should know it wasn't my fault. I always tried to stop her talking about such morbid things, but sometimes she would say things like that anyway.

It was horrible. I found her, and that was bad enough. But it was the guilt that was worse. I felt that if I had only tried a bit harder, or if I had been there more for her that week she might not have done it and then she would still be here now. And then I was angry at her for doing it, and that made me feel even more guilty.

I don't have any positive ending to the story, I'm afraid. I'm gradually trying to get over it and rebuild my life. The one thing I do try to do is to remember her how she was when she was happiest, rather than allowing the worst memories to ruin everything.

Tim, 40
Johannesburg

My father passed away last year. He had been ill with stomach cancer for a few years, so it wasn't a surprise. But it still came as a shock when my sister called to tell me he was gone. He had had a sudden stroke while he gardening so it was very quick.

I didn't think it would affect me so much. We didn't have the greatest relationship when I was younger. But in recent years we had got on better. He was lovely with my two children when they were little and that helped bring us closer together.

He never talked much. He was in the army during the Second World War (he was from New Zealand originally), but he never told me much detail about that. I found myself wanting to ask him questions about that, and about other things that I had never discussed with him. I found myself wanting to ask him what it had been like for him when we were kids, and to share experiences with him. But he was gone, and I couldn't speak to him again.

Until someone dies you always think there is plenty of time for things like that. But you have to talk to people while you can, because once they are gone you have missed the chance.

Lorna, 32
Michigan

I suffer from Chronic Fatigue Syndrome (CFS). Until the year I was twenty-six, I was perfectly healthy, and I used to swim regularly and climb mountains in my spare time.

That winter I suffered from a serious viral illness – it was like the flu, but it dragged on for weeks. I was also going through a stressful time – my mother had died in the fall, and I had to move house in the middle of my illness as my rental agreement came to an end. I can't be sure of the exact causes of what happened later, but stress and viral illnesses are both known to be contributory factors.

I did get over the virus, but later that spring I started to have strange symptoms. My fingers would go numb, and sometimes even my arms and legs would go numb. I kept feeling very cold or hot, out or proportion to real temperature.

I had been feeling like this for a few weeks when one day I was out shopping. I started feeling really cold, and I was looking for a diner or somewhere that I could sit down to rest. But there didn't seem to be anywhere and I started to feel more and more terrible. Finally I stopped, outside a bank. I remember leaning against the window because I was feeling unsteady. Apparently I just fainted and slid down the window on to the ground. I gave my head a bit of a bump as well. I woke up after a while surrounded by strangers, and I couldn't remember anything – not even my own name. The memory came back gradually as I was taken to hospital but the whole experience was one of the most disorientating days of my life.

They did all sorts of tests on me. I went through an emotional rollercoaster as each thing they tested for I became convinced I was dying of, and then the all clear would cheer me up. But all the time I was feeling really ill. My glands became permanently swollen. It is like you are constantly fighting off a really bad cold – your immune is overreacting to everything, and as a result you have constant symptoms of illness. I ached all the time, and found it increasingly hard to do anything.

By now climbing mountains was a distant memory. I

felt exhausted if I had to walk to the local store. And still no one knew what was wrong with me. At the time there had been a lot of stories about "Yuppie Flu" in the paper – CFS had the reputation of being some kind of imaginary disease and it never even occurred to me that that was the problem.

Eventually one day I was out to get some painkillers from the store and I felt so bad I had to stop on the way home to get a glass of water at the diner. There was a lady serving there who asked what was wrong with me. I ended up pouring out my heart to her and she told me that she happened to know someone with Chronic Fatigue Syndrome, and that many of my symptoms sounded familiar.

She even went away and called her friend who gave her the name of a doctor in the next town who had helped with her illness. I ended up getting my brother to drive me over there, and finally he diagnosed me correctly.

It was a relief to know what the problem was, although at the same time it was worrying as there is no real cure for the problem. All you can do is try to contain it and work around it. I had been making myself worse because every time I recovered a little I would start trying to exercise and make myself feel better until I used up every last bit of energy and had a relapse. Now I started understanding how to pace myself so that I could use what energy I had more effectively. I got supplies of supplements such as Evening Primrose and Vitamin C, both of which are reputed to help – my feeling is that it can't do any harm to cover all angles.

And steadily I did get back to the point where I could cope. The illness is always there and may continue indefinitely. That's something I've had to come to terms with. But at least I am finding the ways to manage it, and to get the most out of my life. I can socialize and get about and work so long as I manage my energy reserves with great caution, and keep myself healthy.

One thing that I found disappointing after the diagnosis was the reaction of many of my friends and family. Quite a few of them simply didn't take it seriously. They thought that since I wasn't "seriously ill," all I needed was to be told to pull myself together. It is one of those illnesses that, because it is disputed, and because people don't really understand it, a lot of people don't really have sympathy for.

On the other hand a few of my really close friends really pulled together around me and made sure that they were available to help me through the hardest times. They understand that sometimes I can't get out of the house but need cheering up so they make sure that they come and see me at those times.

My life has been very different both from when I first fainted with the illness, and again from when I finally found out what was wrong. I have had to make many adjustments, both mentally and physically, to my new condition. I can still find a great deal of joy in everyday life, and I don't so much feel that my horizons have been diminished as that I have to make the most I can of what I have been given in life.

Jana, 60
California

My son was killed in a car accident when he was sixteen, fifteen years ago. He was the youngest of my three children. It was a stupid accident. He got in a car with his friend who was too drunk to drive. There were four of them. The two in the back seat were injured, but my son Damon and the driver Scott were killed outright. It was a tiny consolation that it was probably quite fast.

I was inconsolable. I still am. I loved Damon the most of my children – everyone knew that, so it's no secret. Everyone tried to rally round and help, but there's just nothing you can do. You know that every morning for the rest of your life you will wake up and you will be fine for a few seconds until you remember.

Every day I remember him, and I feel just as desperately frustrated and angry now as the day he died. It wasn't Scott's fault any more than Damon's – I don't blame his family because they are going through the same thing as me. They were both old enough to know better.

But on the other hand it was terrible luck. If the car had just skidded slightly differently, if it had all happened a fraction differently he might have survived. One of the worst moments of my life was realizing that I even wished the car had turned around so the two kids in the back seat had died instead. It's an evil thought but sometimes I'd do anything to have him back.

He's frozen in time for me. He's always a kid – I remember him so clearly from when he was a little toddler, through the times when he was growing up and going to school. All his clothes and the way he smiled. But

I never get to see the man he would have grown up to be – should have grown up to be.

I think my family understand my grief. They know I can't get over it, and they try to do the best they can for me, but really I don't think I will ever be able to leave him behind – in one way it is as though my life came to an end the day he died.

Jack
Ontario

My mother died two years ago. I miss her every day. We were always very close, from when I was a little boy, and I spoke to her most days even after I moved away from home. She even got on with my wife, and helped us all the time with our kids, so I saw her all the time.

She got ill quite quickly – she had a really bad chest infection and it turned into a serious case of pneumonia. It wasn't even winter, but for some reason she couldn't fight it off – there were some complications in hospital and she picked up an infection, and she just got worse day after day until one night when I was sitting there with her and she just went.

I believe that she is watching over us. I know that she is with me in everything I do these days, and I am always conscious of whether or not she would approve of the things I am doing.

I'm not sure I really believed in Heaven until she died, but now I have a very clear perception that she is there with God, and that we will be going there to meet her when we die too.

Becky, 56
Halifax

For a long time in my thirties I was constantly ill. I had a problem with my stomach – I would be in paint most days. But the doctors I went to see kept just telling me that it was nothing, that it was all in my head. I think that the fact that I was a housewife meant that they didn't really take me seriously. They just thought that I was being neurotic.

Finally one day in desperation I went to yet another doctor, in the next town. For the first time in my life I saw a female doctor there. She listened very carefully to all my symptoms, then made an appointment for me to go the hospital for some tests.

It turned out that I had a genuine problem with my intestines – there were some cysts that could be removed with a small operation. I had the operation a couple of months later, and while it took me a while to get over the actual operation, I was much better once I recovered. I never had problems with my stomach.

It still makes me angry to think that all those male doctors just treated me like a hysteric and didn't listen. I feel like I wasted years feeling constantly unwell. But I'm grateful to the one who did listen and who made sure that I got the treatment I needed.

Barney, 45
Arkansas

I knocked a woman over while I was driving five years ago. I was changing the tape in my truck and I looked up just as she was walking out into the street. She was looking the other way and must not have realized I was coming.

I tried to brake but it was too late and I hit her hard. I stopped as fast as I could and jumped out. Her friend was there, screaming at me that I had killed her. She wasn't dead – they came and took her to hospital. But she did die a few hours later.

The guilt was terrible. The police investigated and treated me like a criminal, though in the end they decided it was an accident rather than negligence. But I blamed myself. She might have been walking out, but if I had been able to brake sooner or swerve, she might still have been alive.

She had a husband and kids, and every day, even now, I wake up and think about how terrible it must have been for them to lose a wife and mother.

I can't really drive much any more. I quit my job driving because I kept getting scared and panicky. I would just start shaking and have to pull over. It was just an accident but it made me feel like a murderer.

I drank too much for a while as well, and ended up splitting up with my girlfriend. Really my life fell to pieces for a while after the accident.

If it sounds like I'm feeling sorry for myself, that's not my point. My life changed, but I can still turn things around, and I'm still here. That poor woman is gone and her family must still be grieving. I'm not the victim. But it is hard sometimes anyway.

Albert, 40
Brussels

I was diagnosed with cancer three years ago. I was lucky because they caught it very early and it was operable. But it was very frightening to find out that that was why I had been having symptoms.

There were two days that were important. The first was when I was told by the doctor. Cancer is such a frightening word, and no matter how he tried to reassure me, I couldn't really listen because I just thought I would die.

They got me into hospital fast, within a few days. I had to make a will and write letters to everyone I knew who I wanted to leave a final message for. I mean I didn't really have to, but I thought I should in case there was a problem with the operation. And even if I survived I thought it would be better to write these letters now rather than waiting. If I had the operation and survived but was still ill, it would have been difficult to face up to. I wasn't sure if I would be able to cope with that.

It was incredibly emotional. I couldn't write long letters, so I had to try and wrap up everything I needed to say in a few paragraphs for these people who I had known my whole life.

For some people it was just a few jokes and telling them not to worry. For others it was a matter of trying to explain how much they had meant to me. By the time I had written fifteen letters I was an emotional wreck and had cried so many times. I didn't always cry from sorrow – sometimes it was a kind of happiness at remembering good times. They say your life flashes before your eyes. This was more of a slow grind through the whole thing, good and bad.

150

Then I went in for the operation – no one knew except my mother because I didn't want to alarm people unnecessarily. Thankfully I woke up and felt alright. Afterwards they told me that they thought it had been successful but that they had to wait for the result of one more biopsy. This didn't come through until two days later – I had to go back into the hospital having gone home to get the final result.

I knew as soon as I got there that it was good news. The doctor looked too cheerful for anything else, and sure enough I was fine. They had managed to catch it. I have never felt so relieved in my life.

Of course it may come back in future. I have to try and live as healthily as possible to stay healthy as that improves my chances.

The only one of the letters I gave to its intended recipient was the one for my mother, the longest one. It basically told her how grateful I was to her for everything she had done for me throughout my life. The others are with my solicitor as I guess they can go to my friends when I do eventually die, though hopefully that will be a long, long time yet.

My mother called me the night she got the letter. She was really happy with it but she was so overcome she couldn't stop crying on the phone. In the end she had to give up and write a letter back – it was a beautiful letter and I still have it in my wallet – I like to read it now and then to remember the emotional time I went through.

Family Stories

We spend a huge part of our lives as part of the strange little communities called "families". As children we learn our first lessons in life from the way we are raised and the way we are treated by those in our family.

For many, this then leads on to the second phase of familyhood, in which we move on to form family units of our own, with or without children.

A number of these accounts deal with the experience of becoming a parent for the first time. It is an exciting but frightening thing for most people. The responsibility of guarding and nurturing a helpless child has a lasting effect on people's lives and builds a bond that will never fade entirely.

In the last account here, Jade knew her child for only a short time before giving her up for adoption. Nonetheless the bond remained with her through her life, an empty space inside her that she was always aware of.

There are also stories here of families coping with difficulties. Anais' family had to learn how to recover from serious financial difficulties.

Mike's family was tearing itself apart and violence seemed to be the only solution. In fact the account is also a powerful account of a boy learning responsibility and self-respect the hard way. He clearly knows that his actions were the lesser of two evils, which makes his a hard moral lesson for any young man to take.

155

No family is perfect. We all deal with difficulties as they come along, and we all take the lessons that we learn at home out into the world with us. One thing I noticed when going over these accounts was the contrast between the heady optimism of the moments when children are conceived or born, and the more heavy realism that descends on families in later life.

Keeping a marriage together and raising children are difficult tasks and there are no manuals that tell us all the right things to do. The best we can do is to try our best to behave morally and responsibly, and hope to pass our values on to our children.

Thomas, 37
Austria

I remember when I found out that my wife was pregnant. We had been trying for a long time. We'd had to go to the hospital and undergo tests. My wife was convinced that she was infertile because there had been some history of that in her family, a long time ago.

But it turned out to be me. I had a low sperm count, and a high proportion of "lazy sperm". That didn't mean it was impossible. The doctors gave us a list of all the things we could do – lukewarm baths, no alcohol, loose underwear. There are all sorts of things and that's before your friends become involved. People recommend all kinds of vitamins and supplements – old wives stories mostly but you don't want to miss anything in case it's the one thing that counts.

We'd been trying for a couple of years before we even went to the doctor and then a year more of all these things, and nothing. I'd pretty much given up hope and was getting used to the idea we weren't going to be blessed with children.

Then one day at work I was very busy preparing for a presentation and my wife called and asked if she could meet me for lunch. I asked if it was important – I was so busy I didn't even want to break off for lunch. And because she realised that, she just told me on the phone. She said "I think I might be pregnant and I want to talk to you about it."

I had a rush of blood immediately. I just dropped everything. I told my assistant to sort everything out and

157

delay the presentation no matter what. Then I went home.

It turned out my wife didn't just think she was pregnant. She had already done a home test and had it confirmed at the doctors. She had been so worried that it would be a false alarm, she had waited a whole week to have a doctor's test before telling me. I couldn't believe she had kept quiet about it for so long. But she was right. It meant I got all the excitement in one go. It was wonderful to know that it was going to happen after all. We just laughed and laughed when I got home.

Of course we then had to start worrying about all the things that come with pregnancy and babies. It's not a simple thing, just the start of a long complicated road. And of course, ironically, after it was so difficult the first time we ended up having a second child by accident after only another year, so now I have two marvellous sons, and I'm very happy about it too.

Howard, 39
Birmingham

This won't mean much to anyone who hasn't been through the same kinds of experience as me. My wife was pregnant – this was five years ago. She wasn't very well through the pregnancy and I guess I took a lot of time off work. Then the baby was born and it was even more diffi-cult. I only had two weeks of paternity leave and then I went back, but she needed far more help and I had to take a lot of time off work to help out.

In the end I was sacked. Unfortunately I had been there

for a short enough time that they didn't need any excuses. They just claimed that they didn't need me any more. I felt I had been coping as well as I could in the circumstances and I thought it was an appalling thing to do, but I had to cope with it.

It wasn't easy to get another job, and we had to live hand to mouth for a while. We even had to move from our two bedroom flat to a one bedroom flat, which meant that the baby was sleeping in the front room. Once it got past her bedtime we were cooped up in the kitchen and the bedroom with just a little TV to amuse us. It was really hard to cope with on top of being short of money.

I worked in bars and did some temporary bits and pieces. All the time our savings were running low. We had been planning on buying a house after the baby came – little did we realize how long that was going to take.

Finally I got another job, a better one than the one I had left. Still we were stuck in that little flat, coping with the tiny space we had, as we needed to save up a deposit for a house. We had some extremely difficult times there, with bad arguments and some very depressing spells.

Eventually we managed to pull through and get to the point of looking for a house. My job seemed secure enough and we had some savings. We looked around and found a nice little three-bedroomed house with a garden (another thing we had been without in the flat – it was on the first floor with no garden, which made life even more difficult).

We put in an offer, which was accepted and moved within the month. The day we got there was amazing for me. We had worked so hard to get out of the hole we had been in. I picked up the keys first thing from the solicitor and went down to see the house on the way back – the moving van was due in the morning so there was no rush at this stage.

I walked in and the whole house was cleared out and very clean, for which I was grateful. It seemed so huge and had such a happy feeling for me that I almost cried. I walked out into the garden, and it was a beautiful day, and I actually lay down on the grass to look up at the house.

I had a mixture of gratitude that we had managed this, optimism about the future, and pride that we had worked so hard to achieve our aims all wrapped together. I don't think I'd felt so happy in years to be honest.

Of course moving was terribly hard work, and later that day the house was full of clutter and chaos, with Tom, who was four by now, running around like a lunatic chasing the cat. But even thought the serenity I had experienced earlier on was shattered, the happiness stayed with me. And now I had Karen to share it with too.

The moment when I actually cried was when we showed Tom his new bedroom. He knew we were moving, but we hadn't gone on about it too much so he wouldn't be over excited, or disappointed if it fell through. But now he was absolutely amazed that he had his own room. He was wide-eyed, like at Christmas when he saw the presents that "Santa" brings. He immediately started arranging all his toys all round the room and bouncing on the new bed of course, but it was so nice that we had been able to get this for him.

When we finally managed to get him to go to bed it was about midnight. We stayed in there for a while watching him sleep, then turned the light out and came out. We didn't have the kitchen sorted out so I went down the road and bought some takeaway pizza and a few beers. We sat out in the garden on boxes because it was still nice and warm, and we hadn't been able to do this for a long time.

We didn't have to talk too much, we just sat there giggling and pretending we were having a fancy meal. We'd managed to get the bedrooms sorted out, and although there was still loads of work to do, it was such a joy to be here that it didn't really matter.

That day is a very happy memory, and having some real space to live in transformed our life. We became much happier just because there were less reasons to be unhappy. We had space to have friends around to the flat, space to play out in the garden (Tom had been a real handful in a small flat), and space to do all sorts of things. Even if we had a row in the evening, at least we had space to go into different rooms and calm down for a while.

If you've never lived in cramped conditions this might all sound a bit indulgent or trivial, but your life can really be ruined if the space you live in is too confined, especially if you combine that with money worries. We now have a decent space, and even though it costs us plenty of money each month, it is worth every penny we pay and more.

Kath, 58
Saudi Arabia

I discovered a family secret last year. My father is not really my father. My mother had an affair with my Uncle Ken when they were younger. More of a fling than an affair. So Ken was my father, not Dave (my "father").

161

I only found out because my father (Dave, that is) was ill, and started to have gloomy thoughts about dying. My mother died five years ago, and Ken has been dead for two years. He started thinking about what it would be like for me to never know this secret, and for some reason he got more and more guilty about it.

I've lived out in Saudi Arabia for fifteen years now, but I go back most Christmases. So last year, on Boxing Day, he took me out for a walk and told me all about it. He was terrified, poor man, because he thought I would be angry. But I just felt sorry for him.

In truth we had never got on that well. As I got older, I found that we had been closer than when I was young – especially after my mother died, because I was closer to her. It must have been very difficult for him, for them all to keep such a secret from me. I suppose they thought it was for the best. My mother and father got over it and wanted to stay together. We used to see Uncle Ken sometimes but understandably not that often. He did used to send me lovely presents at Christmas though. My father was honest enough to say that that made him angry, or jealous.

We had a good long talk about it, and I told him I understood. Then I came back to Saudi Arabia. But the thing is that I have felt very different ever since. Whenever I think about my life, there is a sense of unreality over it all that wasn't there before. My mother, who I remember as a very generous warm-hearted woman, seems different now that I know the truth. And I feel cheated that I can't talk to her about it.

With my father it changes less, in that we were never so close in the first place. But still I feel very strange about him now. To be honest I'm not sure he should have told me at all. Or they should have told me years ago. But doing it now so late on, when I can't talk to my mother and Ken about it just raises all kinds of strange anxieties and questions that I can't resolve.

My partner has been very good with me this year. He has had to be a bit like a therapist, talking me through all the same issues over and over. He has been so patient. At least I know that my life with him is real and good, so in that respect nothing has changed.

Jane, 30
Bolton, England

I have three children now. I don't know how, as I hate being pregnant and I don't like giving birth one bit. It's uncomfortable, painful and scary, and each time I swear I won't go through it again.

And then just when you have been going through this terrible experience you finally feel the relief of the child being born.

When my first child was born, I remember lying there in the hospital bed, drenched in sweat, exhausted from the experience, and then they put this little bundle in my arms, and immediately I forgot everything. Such a tiny thing, with a perfect little face. It looked perfect to me anyway. My husband was making jokes about it looking a bit squished – he's like that, he'll make a joke about anything. But he was happy too – I could see he was trying not to cry, and then I started crying anyway.

I didn't want them to take her back. I just sat there

163

cradling her, talking to her and telling her how happy I was to see her.

The other two times were similar, but the first time was the most intense because I just couldn't believe there was really a child inside me until she came out, and then as soon as I saw her I knew she was a real little person. You could see right away that she had her own mind (she still does – she's the most stubborn, difficult but lovely little girl!)

It makes you feel everything at once – humble, happy, excited, terrified, confused. But through it all you just feel this intense love and that's the thing that matters in the end.

Anais, 34
Texas

My father went bankrupt when I was fourteen. He was a businessman, and had seemed to be doing very well. A lot of his money was in property and he was doing well out of it. But he had taken too many risks and he ran into a series of problems. He made a big loss on one development which turned out to have a lot of problems and then it escalated from there. Property prices had been going up for years but just at the wrong moment they started to fall, and he was having to chase the market down, selling places at prices that barely covered the mortgage. I don't know all the ins and outs of it, but he had a year of stress before he finally came home one day and told us there was no more he could do.

We had a lovely house with a big garden and swimming

pool. But it was tied to his business somehow, so we couldn't stay there. It had to be sold with the business, and we had nowhere else to go. The day we had to move out was terrible. I went from being a rich kid with everything I could want at home, to being poor white trash overnight. We had to rent a cramped apartment in town, and even then we were poor. My mum who had always stayed home had to go out and find work as a waitress just to get some money together for everyday necessities.

My father was crushed, but my mother was amazing. She was incredibly supportive. She didn't blame him at all. She just took the view that it was his risk taking that had given them fifteen years of luxury, and that somehow they would get out of this mess sooner or later.

I learned a lot from that experience. I had a great respect for the way my parents coped. Even though my dad was devastated, he got straight back out trying to find ways to make us some money so that we could move on. And the way my mum stuck with him was very admirable.

I also learned to cope with great upheaval. Because even though it was a difficult experience, it didn't hurt me in the end. A few of my friends treated me badly because of it. To start with that hurt but then I realized that anyone who only likes you because of your money is not someone you want to be friends with anyway.

I actually suspect I'd be a worse person if it weren't for that experience. I was a bit of a spoilt teenager before that, but because I had to pitch in with everyone to make ends meet, I learned about the other side of the coin. We managed, and after a few years my dad managed to get going again and they bought a nice house outside town again – not as big as before, but at least it was somewhere.

I'd left home by then. I had to work my way through college, whereas I'd always thought that I would be paid for all the way. But at college when I saw the sorts of kids who had an easy ride their whole life, I didn't like them. I liked the kids who had to scrimp and save and work better. Not that there is anything inherently noble about being poor. I don't think that at all. I just think that being rich your whole life makes you take things for granted.

Carl, 33
Leeds, UK

My son Ben was born three years ago. There had been a few complications in the final stages of my girlfriend's pregnancy and I was quite nervous about the actual birth. She went into labour late at night, about three weeks early – in fact she'd been feeling funny all day but it wasn't until she lay down for the night that she finally gave up and admitted she had to get to the hospital. I drove her to the hospital. Because of the complications, even though she was in labour, they had to deliver the baby by caesarian, so they rushed her into the theater, and within about two hours of her deciding to go to the hospital we were there ready to go. I was wearing a gown (the wrong way round, she always reminds me). She seemed calmer than me – though I think she was quite scared.

They had me hold her shoulders while they put a needle into her back – the spine really I suppose. It's quite a scary moment as they have to get it right. After that I was a bit shaky and actually had to sit down for a bit – it was partly that it was the middle of the night and partly the fear.

166

I didn't watch much of the operation – I just sat at her end of the table talking to her. The surgeons and anaesthetist were all very blasé and calm – they were grumbling about being woken up in the middle of the night and asking why the baby couldn't have waited a few more hours.

Eventually the moment came when they pulled the baby out. We didn't know it was a boy until they told us, just before we caught our first glimpse. I'd always wanted a boy, and so had she, so we were delighted.

Then a quick look at the baby held up in the air by the doctor, before they took him over to various contraptions they use to clean and weigh him. He started crying as soon as he came out, and no wonder – it's quite a sudden introduction to the world. But it was a relief because you could hear he was fine and breathing from the start.

Then finally they came and put him next to my girlfriend wrapped in a white towel. She started crying because he looked so beautiful. I felt very emotional but also quite scared because he seemed so tiny and defenceless. It was hard to imagine that we were going to have to look after something so little.

After that it's a bit of a blur. The next day I had to go and buy him a hat and a cardigan, tiny little things that looked like dolls' clothes. The nurses were worried that he would be cold so they had sent me out on an errand, while my wife was hoping to get some sleep. I remember driving along in the car singing that song "Isn't He Lovely" – of course that's not the right words, and it's a cheesy song, but I was very excited and hyper.

That was a huge day for me, very emotional, but really the day my life changed was when we took him home, a few days later. We drove home, about ten miles an hour because my girlfriend was worried about him being rocked about, though it just sent him to sleep.

When we got home I carried him inside and we put him on the middle of the living room floor in his Moses basket. He looked wonderful, so tiny and perfect, and still asleep. And we just stood there. My girlfriend was exhausted as she hadn't got much sleep at the hospital. I wanted her to go to bed, but there was just too much to think about and worry about.

I remember saying, "Now what do we do?" And we had no idea. I mean, we'd read books and been to classes, but that all means nothing when you actually stand looking a real baby. We were terrified we wouldn't be able to cope.

It is incredibly difficult actually. At the start you don't have a minute to yourself – you're feeding and winding and sitting with them asleep on your lap, and getting up in the night and so on. And somehow you cope because you have to.

But your life is just transformed, and as far as I can tell at this stage it never goes back to how it was. Because even when the first difficult bit is over, you are still a parent. You'd still do absolutely anything for them, die for them if you had to.

Until you've got a kid you've no idea how powerful the bond is, but as soon as they're born you know it will be there forever, no matter what happens.

Alice, 44
Canada

When I was seven, I found my father in bed with the nanny. It was bizarre in so many ways. Firstly this was a nanny that I really liked. She was called Jane, and she was very pretty and nice, and she had been really good with me. My parents were both busy, high-powered kind of people, so I ended up spending a lot of time with nannies, and she was one of the nicest we had had.

Secondly, I had no idea what they were doing. I had seen people with no clothes on before, but I had no idea of why they were in bed together like that. They were really shocked when I walked in. I was supposed to be downstairs watching a video. There was a lock on the door to the stairs so they probably thought they were safe, but I had worked out where the key was and how to use it.

You know how little girls are. They try to work things out in a sneaky way, for fun more than anything. I didn't even know my father was in the house, and I just meant to go up and surprise Jane by appearing at the top of the stairs. But when I got to the top, there was a funny noise in her room, so I went to see what was happening.

So they were shocked and tried to cover themselves up. Then my father got his dressing gown and started shouting at me for sneaking around, but Jane told him to shut up, and she got some clothes on and came to comfort me. Then my father changed and started trying to persuade me not to tell my mother.

This was all confusing for me, and quite unpleasant. My father was normally fairly distant but nice with me. But now suddenly I was seeing a completely different side of him. They knew that I was a chatterbox and unlikely to just say nothing. And if I hadn't known what was happening or even that it was wrong, my father's reaction made it pretty clear that they were doing something they shouldn't be.

My father left to go back to work, and Jane went back to looking after me. She was obviously very nervous and tense. I remember giving her a hug because she seemed so upset.

I still don't quite know the story of what happened next. I never talked about it to my mother, but obviously either Jane or my father confessed to her, knowing that it was bound to come out. A couple of days later, Jane was gone. She said goodbye to me, and promised to stay in touch (she never did, incidentally) and I cried and cried because I really did like her.

Then my father moved out too. By now I felt like this was all my fault. I really wished I hadn't seen anything, and I tried to just forget all about it, as though that could make any difference.

My mother was terribly unhappy for a while, but then she met a new man, my stepfather now. We got another nanny, but she wasn't so nice. And then after a while we stopped having nannies because I had got to an age where I could look after myself well enough for short periods, and I was going round to a friend's house after school.

I still feel strange about the whole thing. It was such a period of turmoil, all because I was playing a child's game. And then everything got turned on its head. I suppose I should really blame my father, but somehow it has always felt more like my fault rather than his. And it definitely gave me an uneasy introduction to the concept of sex and romance – I don't think that did me much good at all, though you put all these things behind you in the end.

I didn't magically grow up overnight, but I suddenly was plunged into an adult world and had a shock introduction to ideas of betrayal, responsibility and so on. And guilt, because for a long time I felt guilty about what happened. In that respect I did have to grow up a bit because of what happened.

Annie, 25
Texas

When I found out I was pregnant earlier this year, it was like becoming a completely different person over night. I used to drink and smoke and not look after myself. I had no thought about the future. If I got some money I would just spend it right away, even if meant me going without for the next month. I was plain irresponsible.

Then I accidentally got pregnant. I was feeling a bit strange while I was out at the mall and it suddenly came to me that the way I'd been feeling was a bit like being pregnant. I went straight to buy a test, just to prove to myself that I wasn't, but I was. I was so shocked when I saw that. My boyfriend was as shocked as me. We didn't think we were ready to be parents at all. But we talked to all our friends and family and realized that there would a lot of support for us, and we just had to adjust.

Overnight I gave up smoking and drinking and started eating healthy food. Anything I eat it's like I'm feeding it direct to this little baby so I have to think hard about it.

I started to save every penny I had for stuff for the baby. My boyfriend has to force me to even buy some new shoes now, when before I would have been out spending all the time. I'm just not interested in buying things for myself. Maybe that will change when the baby is born and I'm not this funny shape any more!

And I spent days and days getting the house ready for the baby. My boyfriend laughs at me because I'm always in my cleaning clothes or my painting clothes, feathering the nest, and before I wasn't exactly what you'd call house proud. But now I can't stand a bit of dirt in the house, I need everything to be perfect for the baby. I know when it's born I won't have so much time so I want to get the insides and outsides and backs and fronts of everything in the house right for it now.

Now I'm just a few weeks away and I can't wait. I didn't know you could love them so much when they're still inside you, but it's like this baby is a part of me. I feel it moving around all the time, and I even know it has moods and responds to things happening on the outside. When we play music it moves around like it's dancing in there!

I'm still young, but I feel like I've grown up a lot very quickly. No doubt I've got a lot more growing up left to do once I'm a mom!

Mike, 33
Mississippi

My dad used to hit my mother. All through my childhood we would hear them arguing and screaming, and it would often end with him hitting her. When we were little she'd pretend she'd had a fall, or hit her face on the doorframe or whatever. Then when we were about eight or ten, we'd sometimes see it happening and she'd just shout at us to go away.

Obviously she had terrible problems with self-esteem through this time. It must have made it hard for her to be normal with us sometimes. But in between these arguments, things seemed quite normal, and we even had good times. I always loved my mother absolutely. When I was young I loved my dad too, but more and more I couldn't accept the way he would hit her.

The last straw was when I was fourteen. We had had a family outing in the day – a picnic at the local lake, and things had been going fine. Then after I went to bed I heard them start up again. My dad calling my mum names and insulting her – and she would respond and say the same kinds of things back – I knew he was going to snap in the end because that's what always happened. And I lay there thinking about the way no one could ever stand up to him because he was too big and mean.

Now I was the oldest son. I had three sisters and a younger brother but by now I was the biggest in the house, and I just lay there getting angrier and angrier that there was nothing I could do. Then it started. I heard a crash of something smashing and my mother screaming, and something snapped. I jumped out of bed and ran into the kitchen. My mother was shouting at me to get back to bed, even though she was sitting on the floor with her hands over her head. My dad was standing over her, and was obviously about to hit her again.

I was terrified but I just kept going and punched him really hard on the side of the head. He fell sideways and shouted and I just kept hitting him and hitting him. I'd been lucky to catch him unaware and I was completely wired. I hit him a few more times before my mother jumped up and dragged me off.

He was shouting threats at me, but I could see I had hurt him – his nose was bleeding and one eye was swelling slightly. I was just shouting at him – I told him I was big enough now and that he ever laid another finger on her I'd kill him, and things like that. By now my brother and eldest sister had come out of their rooms and they were standing behind me. I was shouting that he couldn't do that to my mother any more.

He went a bit quiet – I know he knew he could beat me up if he needed to – he could have done it right there, though if he'd touched me, my mum might have killed him. And I think he could see that I was getting bigger, and my brother was only a year behind me. Soon we'd be big enough to really take him on, and we were two sons who loved our mother and would do anything to protect her.

In the end my mother made us all go to bed. He just sat at the table and poured himself a drink and wouldn't speak. I could hardly sleep I was so scared and worried about what would happen next. Once the adrenaline wore off I was just shaking and sweating.

But next day no one mentioned anything. They acted like nothing had happened, and no one even talked to me about it. On the other hand he never hit her again. And about three months afterwards we woke up one day and he was just gone. I never saw him again and I'm glad.

Recently my mother told me she was actually angry at me at the time, because she felt I'd driven him away. She said it took her a few years to really get her self-esteem back and to realize she should have thanked me for wanting to protect her. I don't mind, I'm proud I hit him, and if I ever see him around here again I might do it again.

The other effect it had was to make me much more grown up over night. Until then we had been embarrassed about our home and about what went on there. I kept myself to myself and was a bit weird with kids of my age. But I came out of myself much more after that incident and started to believe in myself.

I'm not saying violence is the solution to all problems – of course it isn't. But there are times when it is the only way you can make a bully stop, and that's what I had to do to my father.

Jade, 44
California

When I was eighteen I got pregnant. It was all a bit of a disaster. It was the result of a one-night-stand that I really regretted.

I realized I was pregnant quite late, which made life difficult. I didn't much like the thought of an abortion in any case. I'm not against it in all cases, but as soon as I thought about doing it seemed like a terrible thing to do for me and my baby. I suppose that once you start thinking of it as a baby it becomes a much more upsetting thought.

But I couldn't keep the baby, or I felt I couldn't. I had no money, no family around me, and I lived a very unstable lifestyle. I suppose I could have moved back home to Colorado and had the baby and stayed home with my parents but that seemed like a terrible idea, as though my life would be over.

I was due to go and visit my older sister in England that summer – she moved over there to work. So what I did was I went and talked it all through with her. After a lot of agonising and discussion, we agreed that the best thing would be for me to have the baby adopted in England and for us never to tell my parents.

So that's what I did. I remember when they took the baby away after the birth terribly clearly. I had tried to prepare myself for this. I had thought about how important it was that I didn't allow myself even a glimmer of attachment to the child. But I was fooling myself. I was already attached to her, even when she was inside me. As soon as I saw her I felt a terrible wrench of my heart, and I couldn't believe that I was doing what I was doing.

But I said nothing and we went through with it. Then a few weeks later I went home to my life in California and tried to forget all about it.

However it stays with you. I couldn't walk past a baby or child without being reminded, and I had a terrible empty feeling in my heart for a long time. I gradually got over it to some degree, but it was always there inside.

Then in my early thirties I got married and had a couple of children. There was some part of me that felt that I was making up for what I had lost. My husband knew all about the baby I had had adopted and understood, but it was still a sore point for me. Now I would see young teenagers while I was out and think about what my first baby was doing and what she would look like now.

My two kids turned out well, one boy and one girl. I enjoyed being a mother, and my life was pretty stable after the turmoil of my teenage years.

Then two years ago, out of the blue, I got a phone call from England. It was a girl with an English accent, who asked for me by name, but it was my maiden name. I had occasionally wondered if this might happen, but I hadn't expected it. But as soon as she asked for me I knew who it was.

I didn't even know her name. She's called Jane. She introduced herself, and it was really hard to know what to say. The first thing I did was to say sorry and to ask how she was. She said she was fine, but she'd always wondered about meeting me. And now she was coming out to California for a conference (she's doing a post-graduate zoology course, so it was an academic thing). It was all quite formal and sensible, not an immediately emotional experience. I think we were both holding ourselves back, because we were scared of it going wrong.

It was the next week that she was coming, so it wasn't long to wait. I gave her all the details and arranged for her to call once she was settled in. Then we said good-bye and hung up. And that's when I started crying.

My husband came through and found me curled in a ball at the bottom of the stairs. I could hardly even talk I was in such a state.

I couldn't even tell you if I was happy or sad. It seemed such a waste of time that it had taken so long. But I was happy she was coming. And scared that we wouldn't get on. He was good about it, and helped me to talk it all over, and I found myself telling him things I hadn't even remembered in years about how it had felt to have her taken away in the first place.

177

The week passed incredibly slowly. Then finally she called and we arranged to meet in the lobby of her hotel. I was terrified but I had to go. And I wanted to do it on my own, rather than with my husband.

I wasn't sure it was her to start with. She doesn't look much like me. She is quite short and dark, whereas I am tall with reddish hair. But there was something about her eyes and mouth that did look like me.

When I saw her and asked if it was her, she just nodded, and then we didn't know what to say. Instead I just held my arms out and she hugged me, and then of course I started crying again.

It's not all easy. This is your child but it is someone you know absolutely nothing about. She told me she'd known my name for years. She'd tracked me down through my sister many years before, but had told her not to tell me as she didn't know what she was going to do about it.

She hadn't told her parents she was meeting me and was worried that they would be upset. I could see that she loved them, and why not. They were the ones who brought her up. But that makes you feel jealous. And then that is such a stupid reaction, as you were the one that gave this child away in the first place, that you feel guilty and bad all over again. Like I said it isn't easy.

But the great thing is that we got on. I was a bit thrown by her English accent. I knew she was in England but for some reason it hadn't sunk in that she would sound like that. She sounded very refined and upper class to me. But she was down to earth and easy to talk to.

She was only out for a week, but we spent several days together. I showed her round a few places, and we had dinner with my family. My kids were amazed to discover

178

they had a big sister, and even more amazed that she was English. But they all got on fine. The last night we went out to a restaurant and then had a few drinks and I finally felt like we were relaxing with each other.

She told me she understood what I had done, which was hugely important for me, because I realize that underneath everything in my life I have always had a layer of guilt about abandoning her. And I started to see that the fact that she was happy and loved her parents was the best possible thing because it meant that I hadn't ruined her life. Rather than feeling excluded by that, I started to feel relieved.

On talk shows and in magazines they talk a lot about closure – I think that's the first thing that we both needed. We had this big empty space in our hearts and heads regarding each other. I knew she was there, and she had known about me since she found out she was adopted when she was twelve. And while we had got on with our own lives, we still had this big question mark there.

Now we had dealt with that, and it made an enormous difference to me. When she left we talked about what we could be to each other. She told me straight that I couldn't ever be her mother. She had a mother already. And while that hurt a little bit, I knew she was right. But we can be friends, and even family, and that's totally important to me. We email each other and phone now and then, and she lets me know how she is getting on.

She has told her parents now and it went fine. They were a bit like me in that their first reaction was a bit of worry that they were being rejected, but she made it clear that they would always be her parents as far as she was concerned.

Now I am planning to go over there for a visit this year. I am looking forward to it. I always wanted to know that she was okay in her life and now I know she is, it is a huge relief, but beyond that I have a special new member of my family.

Near Death Experiences

It is inevitable that a near brush with death will give us a different perspective on life.

These accounts all describe situations in which the teller, or someone close to them, came close to death. The powerful effect this has on our imaginations is well documented. Having been close to death, we tend to think through the consequences that would occur if we were genuinely to die.

And we also tend to reflect on our lives and the way we are living them. Several of the authors of these accounts have taken the experience of a brush with death as a spur to reassess and change their attitudes to life and death in general.

Frank, 44
Bonn, Germany

I nearly lost my wife and child last year. We had been visiting my sister a few miles away, and we were walking down a city street back to my car. My wife and daughter were walking just ahead of me. Elsa, my daughter is four years old, and we have had problems teaching her to be careful around roads. She tends to walk right along the edge of the road, which makes us nervous at the best of times. She is very obstinate. She was walking ahead of my wife.

Suddenly a car screeched around the corner and came careening towards us. I thought maybe it was being chased by another car or something. It all happened very fast. I tried to shout to my wife, and she was looking round at the same time, but right in front of me the car slid across and came quite fast up on to the pavement. It hit my wife Karine with a glancing blow and she fell hard against the pavement and rolled over. She was knocked out, other than that I had no idea how bad it might be. The car rolled right up and ran into the wall, then stopped, with the engine still running.

I couldn't see Elsa at all. I was terrified that she might be under the car. A man got out of the car, on the side away from me, and just started running. I can't believe that even now. It is terrible to not even stop to see what you have done.

I ran around the car and Elsa was lying on the ground, face down the same as Karine. I thought they might both be dead. Someone ran out of a house beside me and said that an ambulance had been called. I ran back to Karine

185

and she was unconscious, with a bit of blood around her mouth and a cut on the side of her head. I could see right away she was breathing, which was something. The woman who had come out of a house knelt down beside her, so I ran back to Elsa.

And amazingly, just as I got there, she was standing up, looking very confused. "What happened?" she asked. "Where's mummy?" It was a complete miracle, but all that had happened was that she had been knocked off her feet and fallen over. Either the car had hit her just as it stopped, or she'd been knocked over by the rush of air behind her back. It must have been the closest escape possible, but all she had was a grazed knee. I grabbed her and picked her up and we ran back to Karine. Elsa was still confused and was telling her to wake up.

Then the ambulance came and we all went to the hospital. Karine was unconscious for a couple of hours, and she was quite concussed when she woke up. She was also in a lot of pain because she had cracked a rib. It took about six weeks to heal and she was uncomfortable for that time. But she was alive.

It changed my life because it made me stop and reassess all my priorities. As far as I was concerned I had seen them die and then they had come back to life. That was how it felt. And now I had them both back I was determined to make sure that I made the best of things. I haven't always been the best father or husband. I can be bad tempered and difficult to be around, and I didn't always do my share around the house. But I've tried to change – I may not be perfect now, but I appreciate what I have and I am trying much harder.

Gordon, 62
Aberdeen

I had a heart attack four years ago. I was the classic case –
too much drinking and smoking, rich fatty food in my
diet, no exercise and a very high stress job. In fact looking
back it's a wonder it didn't happen sooner. But at the time
I thought I was indestructible. You know how it is – you
think heart attacks happen to other people, not you.

It happened on the golf course. I had been feeling a bit
strange since I woke up – short of breath and a bit dizzy.
But I just put it down to a hangover and got on with the
game with my friend Alan. I'd just finished the eighth hole
and as I leant down to place the ball on the ninth tee I had
a flash of strange pain in my shoulder.

I stood straight up and told Alan I needed to sit down –
there was a bench by the side of the hole and I started to
walk towards it. Then suddenly it felt like something had
a hold of the whole left-hand side of my body. I couldn't
speak or react in any way. Alan told me later that I just
went down like a falling tree.

I remember lying there on my back looking up at the
sky. I was sure I was dying – I was trying to say something
to him, to maybe tell Alison (my wife) good bye for me,
but I couldn't talk – it was like when you're in a dream
and something scares you so you try to shout but you just
can't. Alan was shouting at me, asking what was wrong,
and then he was making a call on his mobile.

While I was lying there, I didn't see my life flash before
my eyes, or see a light in the sky or anything like that. But
I did hear this strange mixture of voices and music all
around me – I had the feeling it was the voices of spirits,

but I couldn't hear what they were saying. It was just a cacophony of snatches of sentences and words.

Then I don't remember much. I was extremely lucky because Alan had his phone, and also the hole we were on was only about fifty yards from where a road goes around the back of the course. So the ambulance crew were able to get to me fast and help me. They had to resuscitate me at the scene and again on the way to hospital. I woke up wired up to a big machine, feeling awful, with Alison sitting beside me looking terrified. I was very happy to see her, as I thought I was too young to die. I couldn't talk much or move much at first, but after I'd had some water I did manage to tell her I loved her before I fell asleep again.

It was a few days before they let me out of the hospital, and I got a few stern lectures from doctors and nurses about lifestyle, not to mention my wife going on at me. But really I didn't need it. When you come that close to dying it does make a big impact. You don't need to be told that it will happen again because you know deep down that it will – the indestructible feeling is gone.

I'm no angel – I still have the odd glass of wine, and I eat the occasional rich meal. But I have completely changed my lifestyle overall. I have a lot of salads and healthy cereals as well as taking vitamin supplements and things like that, which I would never have bothered with before. I had to take a lot of time off work after the heart attack, and I was lucky to be able to cut my workload right down to a part-time post after that. I take some gentle exercise every day. I haven't touched the cigarettes or whiskey. And the biggest difference is in my attitude to life. I value the time I have because I know how easily it could be taken from me. I make time for the grandchildren, and I try to stay calm about things that would once have had me in a rage.

I think it was a wake up call for me, and in that I was lucky. I could have died there and then. But I was one of the lucky ones, and I hope that the result will be that I will last a bit longer this time round.

Cally, 34
Montreal

I had a health scare last year. I won't tell you all the details as they're not nice, but I had all the symptoms of bowel cancer, and I had to go for a lot of tests. In the end they weren't entirely sure what was going on so they booked me in for an exploratory operation. They warned me that they might have to remove part of my intestine while they were in there if their worst fears were proved correct.

I looked up a lot of stuff about mortality rates and survival prospects on the internet, and it was very scary. I went around for a couple of months with this hanging altogether over me. All the time I was very cautious about everything in my life, because I felt I might have to rearrange everything around a period of real illness.

When I woke up after the operation, I felt terrible and feared for the worst. But it was all fine. They had in fact removed a small benign growth, but it wasn't cancer or anything, and they predicted a complete recovery.

I felt terrific, as though a sentence of death had been lifted. I feel for anyone who has to go through real illness because while I was very lucky, I found out how scary the experience can be.

My life changed twice, in different ways. First there was the gradual shift to a state of mind where I thought I might be seriously ill. But more importantly, when I found out I had the all-clear, I had a complete burst of energy and excitement. I'd been drifting along in my life for a few years, but now I became completely focused on doing what I wanted to do. I went travelling for three months, and when I came back I still felt totally positive, and I sorted out a lot of things in my life. My good luck was that this scare came at a time when I needed to shift things forward in my life anyway, and it gave me the kick I needed.

Beyond that though, I can't tell you how wonderful that feeling of relief was, when my doctor came in and just smiled and told me everything was going to be fine. I'll remember that feeling my whole life.

Kyle, 48
Los Angeles

I woke up during a major stomach operation. It was a very odd experience. I had severe problems with my digestive system, and they had to operate on me to remove a significant section of colon.

Apparently I lost a lot of blood during the operation and it was touch and go at one point.

How I experienced it was like this. I woke up, and saw all the doctors standing over me, and the lights shining in my face. There was a tube somewhere with blood coming out of it, and a doctor was shouting something.

I was worried because I have heard about people who

wake up during operations and feel everything, but can't communicate to let the doctors know. I thought I might feel terrible pain. But actually that didn't happen.

Instead, I sat up on the table (bear with me, this is all a bit strange . . .) I got off the table and walked across the room. Then I stood there, behind the nurses and doctors, and looked back at all the activity under the lights. My body was still there, so I was looking at them operating on me. The machine was making that flatlining noise that you know from hospital dramas, so I figured I was dead. I was very calm. I looked around and wondered whether to keep walking or go back.

I thought about my wife and kids and didn't want to leave them behind. And maybe that was what persuaded me. It's hard to say really because it was more like I was in a trance, but I turned around and walked back and lay back down.

And then the next thing I knew, I had woken up from the operation. I knew what had happened straight away, but the doctors came and told me that there had been some problems. I asked if I'd been dead for a moment, and they said "Maybe," which I took to mean "Yes."

It was a very interesting experience. It made me realize a few things. Firstly, I know now what happens when you die. You really do become a spirit. I have no idea what would have happened if I'd kept going, but I am absolutely sure that my spirit was able to survive outside of my body, so I believe there is some kind of afterlife.

Secondly it made me realize how fragile life is – as a result I try to treasure the time I have here.

Dev, 54
Austria

I survived a minor plane crash a few years ago. The flight had been fine, but as we were descending to land there seemed to be a problem.

It turned out that the pilot could not get the wheels to lower into landing position. He had to fly around in circles while they tried to sort this out. To start with they just told us that we were waiting for a landing slot, but I could see that the crew were worried.

Then the captain came on the intercom and said that we had a problem. He said that he was going to have to make a crash landing in about ten more minutes. Everyone was very shocked. A few people started muttering prayers. One woman started crying, but no one screamed or anything, even though we were pretty convinced we would die.

They talked us through the safety position, and this time, unlike when we took off, everyone really listened. We all got ready. They also told us that if the landing was successful, we had to get out fast, and made us check where our escape routes were. It was my bad luck that I was halfway in between two hatches, so about as far as you could be from an exit route. I was hoping that there wouldn't be a panic to get out.

The descent was the most frightening ten minutes of my life. We didn't know how far we had to go, or how long we had to live. There was a mixture of muttering and whimpering from around the plane, but mostly we were just holding our breath and praying.

I was on my own, but the middle aged woman next to

192

me, who was also on her own, talked to me a lot, and told me that we would be fine. We held each other's hand on the last descent for comfort. I think she was as scared as me, but she did a great job of calming me down.

We hit the ground hard, bounced slightly, then jolted down again and started sliding. There were terrible screeches and sparks flying up outside. It was terrifying. We just had to brace ourselves and try not to get thrown around. The captain managed to hold the plane in a straight line for a while, then it skidded and went sideways into a field.

Once we had juddered to a halt, I could see what looked like flames outside. The crew started shouting directions and everyone went to the escape chutes really fast, but not in a panic. There was a bit of smoke outside, but I didn't have time to stop and think – I just made it to the chute, jumped in and then ran as far from the plane as I could. I lost track of the woman who was with me, but I know she got off as well, because she was ahead of me in the queue.

There were fire crews coming, and emergency services waiting to meet us. I was shaking like a leaf now, as were most of the others. Looking back, it seemed that the fire was a fairly small problem on the wing. The pilot had actually done a miraculous job of getting the plane down with minimal damage.

There were a few injuries from the landing and a few people had blood on their faces and were being tended to. But I was absolutely fine, except for a stubbed toe and a bruised elbow I had got trying to get out of the place in a hurry.

There's not many days since then when I don't remember how close to death I was. I see it as an inspiring thought. I could have died but I survived. So every day I have is something of a miracle and I should treat it reverently, because I might just as easily have not been here today.

Conquering Fears

Fear can be a rational response to danger. But the fear response in us can also overwhelm our rationality. For the people whose accounts have been included in this section, fear had become a problem. For Thelma, fear was keeping her from doing something that she loved. For most of the others, fear and anxiety had become such a pervasive part of their everyday lives that they were being stymied by anxiety.

It is hard to conquer a fear. No matter how irrational the fear may be, it is hard to rationally put it to one side. Fear is an instinct, and in order to overcome that physiological reaction we need to reprogram our responses.

But if we succeed in conquering fear, the rewards can be enormous. By doing so we can take back control of our lives, and feel that we are in charge and that once again we are capable of self-respect.

Dietmar, 40
Frankfurt

When I was a teenager I was a very nervous person. I was scared of strangers, scared of confrontation, scared of loud noises. I think my mother spoiled me a little as a young child. I was never allowed to do anything risky like ride a bicycle because she was so scared I would hurt myself. I eventually took this fear on myself. I had an unreasonable fear of many things.

This hadn't really improved when I went away to college. To add to it I was quite introverted and withdrawn as well. But I did manage to make a few friends and to mix with different kinds of people. Nonetheless I was intimidated by strangers and by unknown situations.

After I had been there a few months, I was stopped one day in the hall by a girl who was organizing a charity parachute jump. She was stopping everyone, and trying to get volunteers. You had to pay a little money, and then you had to get people to sponsor you. I have no idea why I agreed to do it. She was a very pretty girl, which maybe helped, but I think somewhere in me I knew that it was something I had to try to do.

So a week later I found myself with a group of rather hearty students, undergoing training for jumping out of an aeroplane. It sounds ridiculous, but the training was very calm and even quite fun, and I started to think I could do it. But then I would wake up at four in the morning sweating and panicking about the whole thing, about how stupid I had been to sign up and how everyone would

199

laugh at me if I pulled out – or even worse if I couldn't do it at the last minute.

We went up in the plane on a Saturday. It was a very calm, beautiful day with blue skies all around. I was shaking and sweating, and really didn't believe I could do it. When it came to it, I was only second in the line to jump, which made it worse because I couldn't wait until the end to see if I would chicken out.

I remember standing there with the instructor's hand on my arm, desperately trying to remember everything he had said. I honestly thought I was going to die, but I almost preferred that option to the humiliation of not jumping.

When I jumped it was absolutely terrifying. I won't pretend I really enjoyed it. Some people love the sensation of flying when you freefall, but I was very aware that I was falling, and falling very fast. The moment I did really enjoy was when I was able to pull the cord and feel the parachute jolt up above me, breaking and slowing the fall. That was the first moment at which I didn't feel I was certain to die. Instead I had to concentrate on everything I had learned about how to target the ground and land safely.

Then when I landed, I slightly winded myself but didn't hurt myself at all. And I felt absolutely elated. I didn't want to do it again, but I knew that I had proved something to myself. I had shown that I could stand at the edge of something that scared me, and go ahead and do it anyway.

I always remembered that feeling. I still found strangers and new situations alarming, but I could always remember that I had managed to jump out of a plane, and if I had been able to do that, surely I could do something silly like talking to a stranger, or skiing, or whatever it might be. I wouldn't say that everyone should do something like that but if you are as crippled by fear as I was, it makes a huge difference to prove to yourself that you can overcome the fear, even in such an extreme situation.

Alvin, 55
London

I always used to bury my head in the sand when I had medical problems. My father died of throat cancer when he was in his fifties. He smoked until he became ill, and I spent many years smoking. I have always had the idea that I am likely to go the same way as him.

Last year I started having problems with my chest and throat. It was a terrible burning sensation that would come and go unpredictably, though it was worse after eating and in the mornings.

Of course I became convinced that I had the same thing as my father. I didn't tell anyone this though, no even my wife. Instead I started getting depressed and anxious. I looked up lots of information on the internet about cancer and at alternative cancer cure websites and it just made me more scared and anxious.

It got really bad. At one point I had an anxiety attack in the supermarket. I couldn't breathe, and had to sit down – someone became so convinced that I was having a heart attack they were trying to call an ambulance, but that only made me more scared and I ended up abandoning the shopping and struggling outside.

When I got home I told my wife that the car had broken down and that I was going to have to call out a mechanic. It's pathetic in retrospect but I was backing myself into all these corners to avoid facing up to what I imagined was the truth about my health.

But that led to things changing. My wife, without telling me, went outside and checked the car. She had become quite concerned about my behaviour, but actually she had convinced herself I was having an affair, because that was the only explanation she could think of for how odd I had become in a couple of months.

So she confronted me and I finally had to own up to the fact that I thought I might be dying. It was a huge relief for me to tell her and she was pleased I wasn't in fact having an affair. But she was livid that I had been hiding this and not going to the doctor to get checked out. She made me promise to do that. And she drove me there herself and sat with me to make absolutely sure that I didn't chicken out.

I was petrified, but the doctor was very calm and went through everything. At the end of the examination he booked me to come back for some tests. He said he was 90% certain it wasn't cancer, but that he would do a couple of tests for safety. He told me that his diagnosis was acid reflux. I'd never heard of it, but it is basically just severe heartburn, where acid from your stomach is backing up into your stomach and oesophagus.

I can't tell you the relief I felt. I thought I was dying one day, then the next I found out it was something quite simple. You just need to eat differently, and I found that tilting my bed at night was also useful. But the main thing is that I wasn't dying.

I've finally come to realize that my morbid fear of death and illness is a bigger problem than any real illness, so I've tried to address that. I even went to see a therapist that my wife found, because she thought I needed to talk to someone other than her about it, and I found it surprisingly helpful. I'm glad I listened to her, she was right – she usually is, but don't tell her I said that!

Alison, 32
Tennessee

I had a period in my early twenties when I became extremely depressed and anxious. I would have these terrible anxiety attacks, crippling ones where I couldn't breathe, and panicked that I was about to die.

I got to the point where I could hardly go out of the house. Even going to the store would take me all day. I'd have to start getting my courage up from when I got out of bed, and it would be hours later before I made it.

What was I scared of? Everything. Strangers, cars, buildings falling down, terrorists, muggers, strange animals. It was an all-encompassing fear.

My family tried to make me go and see a therapist, but I wouldn't show up for the appointments – it was too hard to go.

Eventually a friend of mine found a local therapist who was prepared to come round and see me. I was reluctant, but I knew that I needed to do something.

The therapist turned out to be a woman only a few years older than me. To start with I thought, what can this woman possibly do for me. I suppose I would have been more impressed by an old man with a beard . . .

But she was incredible. The biggest idea she gave me, right from the first session, was that fear is only an idea in my head. She made me talk about the things that scared me – like if I went to a shop I would be scared of muggers. And then she talked about how a normal fear response would be to be scared of something that actually happened. But my fear response was being triggered by an idea of something that might happen.

She made me see that the fear was real, but it was created by something in my own head, and what I had to do was to break the connections that made fear happen.

Then she gave me a program of things I had to do each day or week between sessions. It was basically a series of little challenges – get my hair cut, go to the store on the next block, and so on. It became a bit more challenging each week. And she was very patient when I couldn't manage something. Instead she would focus on what I had achieved, and after a few weeks of this positive approach, even I started to notice a difference.

It became a kind of mantra for me "fear is only an idea in your head." Whenever I got scared, I would try to pause and think about that. And the very act of taking that step back often helped. It didn't always help, but as I found less things scared me, I found that I could work through the fear on the occasions when I couldn't conquer it.

Looking back I can hardly believe how feeble I was at my worst. These days I am much better balanced. I occasionally have minor relapses, but I know I made it through the worst of times, so I know I can manage anything that might come along now.

Thelma, 45
Chicago

I was a singer from an early age. I used to sing at church and then in a band and I always loved it. When I was twenty-three I had my first child and I didn't perform for a year. It seemed like longer than a year because when you are looking after a little kid you lose track of everything that is going on out there in the real world. Then I had the opportunity to go and do some shows with a band who needed a stand-in singer for the week.

The rehearsals went well enough, and I thought it would be fine. But an hour or so before the first show I started to get scared. I had never in my life suffered from stagefright. But I was feeling really bad about going up on to a stage and singing. Maybe it's because as a mother you are in the background and you stop expecting anyone to pay attention to you. It just seemed presumptuous to stand up there and expect anyone to listen to me.

I tried to get over it, but when I got on the stage I was shaking all over. My foot in particular was out of control. Every time I moved one foot I could feel the other shaking. So I just stood rooted to the spot, where normally I would be off around the stage.

It got slightly better through the set, but I was a long way below my best. The band noticed too, although they were nice about it.

I tried hard that week to get over it. I did everything I could think of to relax. But everytime I took a step onto the stage I would start shaking and panicking again. It becomes a vicious circle, where even if you're not scared of singing, you get scared of being scared, and that sets it all off again.

I made it through, but I vowed never to do it again. Then after a few months I was persuaded to do one more show with the same band (they were desperate). I went to the doctor and he gave me some beta-blockers, which are supposed to at least stop the shaking.

They did, but I still had a dry-mouthed panicky feeling all the time. The bottom line was I wasn't enjoying singing anymore. So I gave up. It seemed like singing was just something I had done as a kid, but that I had now grown out of. I had two more kids and I got on with being a mother and doing some work in between.

Every now and then, I would feel sad about it, but I convinced myself it was for the best.

Then a couple of years ago my sister got married. It was a great party afterwards, with a good band. My sister is a few years younger than me, and she never stopped nagging me about how much she liked to hear me sing, and why didn't I sing any more?

Finally at the wedding, she got her way by getting up on stage and announcing that I was going to sing. She had the band play "Natural Woman," which is one of my favourites, and there was no getting out of it.

I don't know what made the difference. It may be that it came out of the blue, or that I was relaxed at that moment, but I went up on stage, and I had a fantastic time. No fear, no stagefright, nothing. It felt exactly like I used to feel when I sang, which was wonderful. My voice still felt good, even though I had only been singing in the bath lately.

It felt so good, I stayed on stage, and did a few more. Then when the singer came back I stayed up there and did backing vocals. I was on stage for the best part of an hour, and I loved every minute.

My kids were amazed, they hadn't really heard me sing before, except for lullabies and that, but not really sing like I could. More importantly the band were impressed and offered me some work. And because I felt so good I said yes.

And that's how I started singing again. Now I do a few nights a week all over the place and I can't believe I ever stopped because I enjoy it so much. In fact I probably enjoy it more than I ever did, because now I really appreciate what a blessing it is to have a voice and to be able to use it. I've never once been scared since that wedding, so I've got my sister to thank for fixing my problem.

Lessons of Age

My grandfather once said to me that the day he started thinking he had nothing left to learn would be the day he became an old man. He was in his seventies at the time.

He also used to lecture me about the arrogance of youth, and about how young people think they know everything. He believed passionately that you have to keep an open mind and a curiosity about thee world around you throughout your life. He lived to a grand old age and was one of the liveliest, funniest men you would ever hope to meet.

The accounts in this section all focus on the same thing. In each case the teller has come to realize something that at a younger age they would not have been able to comprehend. In this respect this chapter is partly about the wisdom of age.

But it is also about keeping an open mind. If Henry had not taken a step back and observed his son closely, he might never have shaken his belief that the son was belligerent and immature. But by observing and thinking he came to a greater understanding not only of his son, but also of himself.

In modern society we often underestimate the wisdom of age. Traditionally we respected the wisdom of our elders because we understood that they had experienced more than us. But these days it is more common to rate youth and vigour over experience and to jettison the valuable contribution that our elders can make. Grandparents are less appreciated within a

211

*family unit that has become more nuclear than
extended. And within the workplace, age is not
respected as it would once have been.*

*The stories of Edgar and Gina show us something
else – no matter how experienced we are, we have new
lessons to learn and new challenges to cope with as we
grow older. In each case, they speak of a time in life
when the changes that have taken place have made
them reassess their place and purpose. We can learn
from the way that each of these people seems to be
dealing positively with the new challenges that life has
brought them.*

Gina, 55
Sydney, Australia

My third child finally left home two months ago. After twenty-eight years of being a full time mother, I found myself free to do whatever I wanted.

I had spent all that time cooking all their meals, keeping track of where they were going out to, making sure they had everything they needed ready in the morning. Then towards the end I was teaching them how to survive on their own – how to cook, clean, wash clothes for themselves and so forth.

Keith, the youngest, was the last to go. He stayed here right up until the summer he left college. I thought he might never leave to be honest! In a way I didn't want him to – I knew I'd be sad when the day finally came. But eventually he got himself a job and a flat and moved out. He'll still be home for some food often enough, unlike the others who live further away and I only see at Christmas or family occasions. They all seem to be doing well on their own though. I am proud of them all, though I'm sure I will still worry about them all as long as I live.

The day Keith left, after my husband left for work, I just sat at the kitchen table. I felt strange – emotionally exhausted. It's not quite sad, because I'm pleased to have the extra time. Of course in the last few years I haven't had quite so much to do, and I have had more time to myself. But somehow until it is a permanent arrangement you feel the same about things. Only when he left did I finally sit down and think, "What next?"

I have plenty of plans for things to do with myself. But

to be honest at this stage I am just taking some time off. It's not the same for my husband. His life hasn't really changed at all. He still goes to work and comes home at night. But he knows I'm at a bit of a strange time in life, and he has been taking me away for weekends, and we went down to the coast for a couple of weeks just to relax.

I know my life has changed – I'm just not sure exactly how yet. I'll let you know in another year or two.

Edgar, 72
Perth, Australia

I broke my hip a couple of years ago. I had to move in with my son and daughter-in-law as a result.

I had never really felt old until that happened. I always just got on with life and did whatever I wanted to do. It was a silly accident. I'm afraid I had had a few beers and on my way home I just tripped over my own feet. I fell badly and knew as soon as I went it was a break. It hurt like hell.

I just lay there on the road while my friend Eddy called for help. The doctors patched me up and sent me on my way. But I needed constant help for a few months. And even once it healed I was persuaded that I can't go back to my old ways.

It's not so bad in a way. You spend your life being terrified of becoming an old man. Then you realize it has crept up on you anyway. My family are marvellous, and I'm a lucky man to have them. I do still get around, and I still have a few beers, but I make sure I have my stick or a few friends to lean on!

But I am old now and I can no longer ignore it. There are things I do need help with. I can't lift boxes anymore, and some days the stairs aré a bit of a challenge. That's what changed – although it had probably already happened – it just took a fall to make me realize.

I haven't had a bad life, and I have good people around me now, so all in all it could be a lot worse.

Colin, 45
Christchurch

It's not the worst thing that could happen, but my hair went gray overnight more or less. One day, two years ago, there were a few gray streaks here and there. The next day most of it had faded, and the day after that I was gray.

I was single at the time (divorce, long story . . .) and the first effect it had on me was to make me feel depressed. I felt that I had gone from being someone who could pass as thirty-something to an old man overnight. Now no one would ever date me.

But I also just felt that my body was overreacting to something and that the stresses I had been through had made me age dramatically. Actually apart from the hair I didn't feel too bad, but all the little aches and strains that you start to feel more as you age became suddenly very significant.

All my friends and family just laughed at me, except my mother who was sympathetic.

But actually once I got over the shock it wasn't so bad. Maybe I was exposed to the thing everyone goes through in becoming middle aged, but in a short sharp shock. I realized I just had to accept that I wasn't young any more. But I didn't feel so bad, and I was still happy in my life for the most part.

You just have to adapt. I'm not looking forward to being actually old, but I suppose you adapt and change as you go along.

I do actually have a girlfriend again now. She's a few years younger than me, and she says my hair makes me look distinguished, so I think I should be pretty happy with that!

Kyle, 67
San Francisco

The thing about everyone remembering where they were when the heard that Kennedy had been shot its such a cliché, even though it's true. I don't think the younger generation can really understand the sense of shock we had about it.

Looking back, I think we pinned too much hope on Kennedy. It was a very optimistic time. We had come out of the 1950s, and there was this real feeling that his youth and positivity represented something that was in the air. We were moving on into a new age and it was going to be a better one.

Then he was shot. My girlfriend woke me up from a nap to tell me about it. I wouldn't have believed it if she hadn't had such a white face. It was as though all the color and joy were suddenly draining out of the world.

I still don't know who wanted him dead, but I do know

that there were dark forces at work that didn't want the same things that the younger generation wanted. They certainly didn't want any of that love and peace stuff. And look at what happened afterwards – Vietnam, and the other assassinations, and the Chicago riots and then on to all the chaos of the early 70s. I think that all suited certain vested interests very well. It still makes me shudder when I think about the fact that even Eisenhower warned about the military-industrial estate, but no one really listened.

But what I see now is that we pinned too much on Kennedy. Maybe Vietnam would have happened anyway. He had his faults, and they might have become more apparent over time. Young people think they have discovered the world for the first time and that their parents are fools. But that's not true now and it wasn't then. The old people that we all despised for being square were the generation who had survived a world war. Maybe they actually knew a bit more about the world and the way that things move in cycles than we did. We were innocent, which is good, but we were naïve too.

I was thinking about this recently. I knew some young people who had very extreme reactions to 9/11. Now that was a similar sort of event to Kennedy dying in that it was a hugely traumatic news event, which shaped a lot of people's perceptions about the world we live in today. There were some who wanted a very aggressive kneejerk reaction from the U.S. (which is pretty much what they got of course . . .) Others drew sweeping conclusions about conspiracies and dark theories about the world.

The thing is, the world is more complicated than we can understand. It is likely that with Kennedy and with 9/11, there are things that we will never know about what really happened. And it's likely too that there was a degree to which the official stories were true.

But this time I have the experience to take the long view, to treat official announcements sceptically, without immediately jumping to the opposite conclusion. I was upset and hurt by 9/11, but it didn't shape my world-view in the way that Kennedy's death did. And I think that that is a matter of age and experience.

Henry, 58
Philadelphia

My eldest son had his first child last year. He got married a few years ago and I wasn't sure that they would ever have children. I always worried about him. We have two younger children, a daughter and the youngest son, who are both much more carefree and easy than him. He was always rebelling against me when he was younger. I can understand that but it made life difficult sometimes.

And I thought that his belligerent attitude might make life difficult for him. He got fired from at least two jobs, and it was mainly because of his attitude so far as I can tell. When his wife became pregnant I was worried for them.

I didn't see him much during the pregnancy, though we spoke on the phone a few times. He sounded nervous, and even asked for my advice once or twice, which is very unlike him.

After nine months we got the call to go down to the hospital. The baby was a girl, a lovely looking child, with beautiful blue eyes. She reminded me a lot of how he looked as a tiny baby.

He was so proud. He was there holding the child, fussing over his wife, and bossing all the nurses around. Later on we had to go back to the house with him, while his wife stayed the night in hospital with the baby – we were going to pick her up in the morning after a few more tests.

Back at the house he told me all about his new job, and it seemed like he was determined to make a go of it. And then he started showing me how they'd set up the house. He'd decorated the nursery and built a cradle, and everything was childproofed and perfectly prepared. They'd obviously spent a lot of time and thought of everything. In fact they'd thought of things we'd never even done when he was little. I found myself wondering how we'd ever got through three childhoods without a single safety gate!

The thing I'm trying to say is that I realized that he was going to be fine. He had grown up to be a fine young man, and he was going to be a good husband and father. Not that I really doubted it, but at times I had been anxious because he had seemed so mixed up. But now I could just relax and let him be the one in charge.

It was a lovely feeling seeing him there – it reminded me of myself at the same age, in a way that made me wistful and proud at the same time. Finally all the difficult years we had had seemed to make sense and I knew that I would be able to enjoy being a grandfather. I'm looking forward to being the one who gets to play games and buy presents while the parents do all the difficult stuff!

It's also the moment when I finally felt that my time as being a parent was over. Always at the back of my mind I had been prepared to go back to being the stern dad, or to bailing them out when they were in trouble, but finally I'd got past that. It means I'm a bit older, but a bit happier in my life.

Lessons
From Strangers

From an early age we are subjected to a barrage of advice from all quarters. Our parents and teachers tell us how to behave. As we grow older, self-help gurus, religious leaders, politicians and talk show hosts take turns to lecture us in how we should live. Even advertisements and lifestyle makeover shows these days are full of messages about the right lifestyle.

Small wonder that we turn off and stop listening sometimes. You can't take every piece of advice on board. So you have to select and filter what you are told. A lot of the time the only option is to ignore all the advice.

But sometimes when we are in need, we listen and some advice comes through and makes an impact. Surprisingly, often we can learn something from someone we have never met before. Because we have no preconceptions about a stranger, their words sometimes strike home in a way that the words of those close to us don't – we set up defences and preconceptions about the people who are around us everyday.

Most of the people whose stories are included in this section had a problem in their life that they needed to deal with, whether it was something they were consciously or subconsciously aware of. Even Alfie, for whom there is no obvious problem, seems to be aware of the fact that his own reactions to provocation were inadequate and involved him in a loss of control. Reading between the lines, this is why the stranger in his story made such an impact – because he taught him

223

a completely different way to respond to being provoked.

The fact that they were dealing with problems may have made them more receptive to the lessons that these strangers had for them. However any time you learn a lesson about yourself, you need at some level to have an open mind. As long as you go out into the world every day with all your mental defences intact, it is hard to discover anything new about yourself. But if you manage to take a step back, and look at yourself through a stranger's eyes, you will often find the first step towards improving your self-awareness and overcoming problems in your life.

Alfie, 60
London

I was sitting on a train once, quite late at night, when I was younger (this would be about thirty years ago now). The ticket collector came down through the train checking tickets as they do.

The man opposite me was a bit older than me. There was a problem with his ticket. He had a ticket from somewhere down in Surrey (Haslemere I think) to London. He had missed the last direct train and had asked the platform staff what he could do. They had told him to go via Brighton, which he could do if he jumped on a train going the other way and changed. He had done this.

Now the ticket collector was telling him that he wasn't allowed to do this on the ticket he had. He explained that he had bought the ticket in good faith and had only done what he was told by the station staff.

Then the ticket collector started asking him for more money – he wanted to charge him the extra for going by a different route, and it was quite a lot more.

The man stayed calm and repeated what he said the first time. At this point the ticket collector became angry and started shouting, but it made no difference – the man remained perfectly calm and unbothered.

Then the ticket collector went away and came back with a colleague, the train manager, and they went through it all again. They started threatening to make him leave the train at the next stop if he didn't pay, which I thought was an outrageous threat given the circumstances. I was becoming quite angry at them, and tried

225

to interject on his behalf. But he really didn't need any help.

He stayed serene, eventually giving them his address and asking them to send a copy of the paragraph in their rules and regulations that gave them the right to charge more in this circumstance, and also of the rule that allowed them to threaten to evict him. He also, while they were still there, asked for my address as a witness, and asked for their names, which they gave only reluctantly. In the end after all this nonsense, they backed down and said they would let it go this time, but he shouldn't do it again.

After they left I asked him how he had managed to stay so calm in the face of such belligerent idiocy. I knew for a fact that if I had been in his place I would have been shouting too, and it might even have ended in a fight.

He said that he had got angry about things like that when he was younger, but he had eventually concluded that if he got angry, he stayed angry all day, and then he had allowed someone else to ruin his day.

By staying calm, he said, he was able to remain in charge of himself, and therefore act more effectively. And more importantly he was denying them the right to control his life by ruining his mood for the day.

I was extremely impressed by his attitude, and also by the thought that reacting to other people in the way they want you to is allowing them to control your life. It's something I took away with me into my whole life. I do a lot of quite difficult negotiation meetings in my career, and I have often stayed calm in extreme situations by remembering how well he coped with those idiot train guards.

And in my private life, I also started to stay calm in situations where I might previously have lost control. In particular I found it to be a useful lesson once I had children – both with toddlers and teenagers, they spend a lot of time trying to make you angry just to get a reaction. I won't swear that I always managed to stay calm, but the more I did the more I found I was able to stay in charge.

And also, with kids, they respect you more if they can't rile you into losing your temper. It's paradoxical, but if you don't do what they want, in the end that's more valuable for your relationship with them than if you give in and get dragged into pointless arguments and shouting matches.

Malcolm, 44
Edinburgh

I used to have a problem with drink. But I didn't see it as a problem at all. I enjoyed drinking. When I was younger I used to get drunk with my friends every weekend, and it was fun. It was a release from everything.

Then as I got a bit older I became more regular. I would rarely skip a day. I didn't always drink enough to have a hangover, but I'd almost always have a few glasses of wine or a few cans of beer. Even at that point I don't think it was a real problem in my life, but I was certainly becoming dependent. My reaction to every bit of stress, or good news, or just boredom was to break out a drink.

In my early thirties I got married to Sue. She drank in

227

the same sort of way as me, so we were quite compatible in that respect. She was a good girl, and probably better than I deserved. I had quite a stressful job at that stage and I drank more heavily in response.

Rather than having a few drinks, I used to drink until I was unconscious. Then, increasingly, this started to affect me during the day. I would have terrible hangovers and found it hard to do anything in the morning. Then at lunchtime I would have to go to the pub in order to settle my nerves.

Sue used to tell me I was turning into an alcoholic. But for some reason it never bothered me. I suppose I saw it as being in some way tough to drink a lot, and the idea of being dependent didn't really put me off. The first step to being an alcoholic is supposed to be when you admit to being one. But for me that wasn't ever going to be enough. I could call myself an alcoholic and wear it like a badge of pride.

Eventually of course I lost my job. Sue was very good about it and was amazingly supportive. It was afterwards that things became difficult. I was supposed to be looking for new work, but I was still drinking. One day when I had spent the day in the pub, and was drunk by six o'clock when she got home, she gave me an ultimatum. She said I had to give up drinking completely until I got a job.

I tried. For about two days I drank nothing. But then the craving got the better of me. I got really angry at her for not understanding that I was under stress and needed a drink to relax, and went off to the pub again. And because I knew I shouldn't be doing it, I drank even more than usual. I was virtually unconscious by the afternoon.

Even that wasn't the last straw. She gave me chance

after chance and I wasted them all. Eventually she moved out. It was a terrible day in my life, but at that stage I still blamed her. It seems absurd now, but I thought she should be standing by me.

Of course my reaction to her leaving was to keep drinking. I managed to get a few temporary jobs to survive. I'd work a week or two at a time, then go back to drinking.

The real turning point came a couple of months later. I was in a pub in town in the afternoon, and I started talking to this old bloke. I'd seen him in there before – he used to come in the afternoon, and buy one drink, then sit doing his crossword. He might have one more drink about an hour later, then at about five o'clock he would set off. It interested me because he seemed so set in his ways. Most people you see in the pub in the afternoon are serious drinkers, but he was very measured.

So I was talking to him, and he asked me about my life. I told him all about how my wife had left me, just because I liked a drink now and then, and about my job and everything.

He told me that he had been an alcoholic when he was younger, and that it had ruined his first marriage. He didn't give me a lecture about drinking at all. But he told me that he hadn't been able to give up until he was fifty, and that it had taken him ten years to even be able to go back into the pub for a quiet drink for fear of relapsing.

Now he was married again, and he knew he could trust himself to come in for a couple of hours. "I like pubs," he said, "but I don't like what they did to me." He told me that before he gave up, he had realized that his entire life was being dictated by the desire to drink.

At five o'clock, he got up and politely shook my hand, and wished me good luck. That was all, but for some reason that conversation was the one that finally got through to me. I realized that my life was being dictated by alcohol. I went back over everything that happened comparing what I wanted to what happened, and in each case I realized that the alcohol had been the problem. And finally that made me see how right Sue had been to try and make me give up. My drinking had been ruining her life as well as mine. If I chose drinking over trying to make things better, that just proved that I was being controlled by the addiction.

What I realized that day was what addiction really means. It's not just a matter of repeatedly doing something that makes you feel good. It is a compulsion that overcomes your better will. The old man had said it took him until he was fifty to quit and had nearly totally ruined his life. I realized I didn't want to be sat there saying the same thing in thirty years time. I'll always be grateful to him, though I don't know his name because by just telling me his story without lecturing, he made me really take a look at my own life.

I quit that day. It was extremely hard. I had to do all sorts of things to try and divert the urges. I missed the pub terribly, but couldn't allow myself to go. I started doing a lot of exercise, not to get fit, but just for something to do when I was feeling twitchy. The physical addiction was hard to get past, but the mental addiction was even harder. But I kept at it, and kept at it. Once or twice I had a relapse and had a few drinks, but I didn't enjoy it because I felt so miserable about failing, so each time I managed to get back on track.

I started trying to persuade Sue to come back to me but she had moved on to a new man, and who can blame her. That was a difficult period, because I felt hopeless about my future.

But I knew that going back to drinking was the worst thing I could do, and I kept trying. Eventually I got a decent job and met a new girl (Jane – we're married now, with two lovely children).

I was very lucky. I could have wasted my whole life at the bottom of a beer glass, but I managed to pull myself up just in time to rescue things. I can even have the odd glass of wine now without it being a problem, but I always say no to too many. I remember how it ruined my life last time round, and I'm not going back there.

Cathy, 34
Nice

When I was sixteen, I got some work as a model. It was through a friend who suggested me to the agency, and I was lucky enough to be taken on to their books. I didn't really want to be a model, but the pay was quite good and I met a lot of interesting people. The only bad thing was the condescending way that people treated me when they found out I was a model. "Oh, a model," they'd say, and you could see they thought that made me a stupid bimbo. Actually I had good grades in my exams and wanted to do something more interesting eventually, but at the time it was fun. I didn't even think I was that pretty, I just happened to have the kind of face that photographed well.

My parents used to spend a lot of time cautioning me to

231

be cautious in life. They were telling me to save all my money from modelling for a deposit on a house, and if I talked about going abroad to work they always looked horrified. Some of this attitude rubbed off on me. I was ambitious and wanted to do things, but there was still an element of fear. My plan at that stage was to finish school and then maybe do a bit more modelling to try and save up some money.

One day I was on a shoot at the beach. We had to set off at about three in the morning and I was exhausted. I probably had to spend a couple of hours in make-up just to make me look awake!

The woman who was art directing the shoot was very glamorous. I don't know her name, but she worked for one of the big international labels. I told her that I had been offered a couple of month's work in Milan, but I wasn't sure about it because I wanted to finish my school year before I went anywhere. She was funny – she just said, "What do you want to do in life darling, sit in a backstreet making buns, or go exciting places. If someone offers you something exciting to do, grab it with both hands. You're young, you think this kind of thing happens all the time, but it doesn't. You have to grab life with both hands – you only get one chance at life." And then she was off shouting at the photographer again.

It was the idea that this might be my only chance that hit me. I decided that I could come back later and be sensible if I needed to, but in the meantime I took the work in Milan. And that led on to a few more things, in Tokyo and back in London, and for a few years I was on this extraordinary merry-go-round. To be honest I loved every minute. But beyond that I kept that principle in everything

I have done since. You only get one chance at life, so don't put things to one side and hope they will still be there later. You just have to make brave choices and go for what you want.

When I finished modelling I bought a flat and went back to college, and got back to a more "normal" sort of life. But I set up my own business as soon as I could because I wanted to be in control of my own life, and that was also something I learnt from modelling.

Allie, 42
Chicago

I was smoking in a diner once when I was twenty-five. I had two cigarettes with my coffee. It was quite crowded, and I was sitting at the same table as an older man. He looked quite wealthy – he had a nice suit and a nice looking briefcase with him. He looked like he was maybe a businessman, but not something especially formal like banking. Maybe something in the entertainment business, I don't know.

He finished his coffee and started to stand up. I happened to catch his eye, and he sat back down – I thought he was going to hit on me actually, so I got ready to be defensive.

Instead he said that he hoped I didn't mind him observing, but he noticed my smoking. He told me that at my age he had smoked about twenty a day. Then one day he had tried to sort his finances out. He had sat down and gone over all the things he wasted money on, and top of the list was cigarettes.

He pointed at the two stubs in the ashtray and asked me how much they cost me. I said, I don't know, perhaps twenty cents. So he said, think about it. Twenty cents, ten times a day is two dollars, seven days a week is fourteen dollars, fifty-two weeks a year is seven hundred and something. Wouldn't that make a difference in your life?

He said that once he started adding all the little things up to see what they cost him over a year, he got a much clearer idea of what he really needed. He said he was prepared to spend a few hundred dollars a year on his morning coffee because he felt it was an important part of his day. But the cigarettes had gone, along with a few other things. He told me that in the end he had paid off his mortgage ten years earlier and had never looked back.

Then he said goodbye and went away. But he had planted the seed of an idea in my mind. I went away and did exactly the same thing as him. I started to work out the real annual value of things like the sandwich I bought at lunchtime instead of making my own, the cigarettes (I gave them up right away), and the extra bus I got instead of walking a few blocks home. It made the biggest difference, not just to my life, but how I valued the things I spent money on. And like him, I paid off my mortgage early, last year in fact.

I wish now that I knew who that man was, because I didn't really thank him for his advice – I think I just gave him a bit of a confused smile. But in the end it has been the most valuable thing that anyone has ever told me.

Frederick, 30
Boston

I wanted to kill myself when I was twenty. I had a lot of emotional problems, and I was doing drugs that made a bit of a mess of me. I had been in a self-destructive phase of my life, where I wrecked all the relationships in my life and my parents had pretty much disowned me.

I just didn't want to go on any more. I couldn't see the point, and every morning when I woke up I didn't want to be alive.

I went up to the bridge over the river, and I was planning on jumping. It was about dusk on a winter evening, and I walked up there and stepped over the wall that separated the road from the edge. I climbed up the fence and I was just putting my leg over to get ready when someone stopped their car and ran over. For a moment I kept trying to climb, but he grabbed my foot, and then asked me what the hell I thought I was doing. "Jumping," I said. "Not as long as I'm here," he said. He had a good hold on my foot, and he was pretty strong. It was a guy who was a few years older than me.

I gave in and got down, figuring I could wait for him to go away and try again. But he kept talking to me and asking where he could take me. I said there was no one I wanted to see.

So instead he said he was going to buy me a coffee and talk to me. He made me get in the car with him and drove us a mile down the road to the diner. It was pretty much empty and he bought us coffee and pie and sat me in a booth at the back and asked me to explain.

He seemed a nice guy and he was a good listener. So I

found myself telling him all I could about it. The drugs, the friends, the relationships, all the family stuff. I explained how I'd been burning all my bridges.

He said that it made him mad to think of someone like me, with my whole life in front of me throwing it away. He said that whenever he drove over that bridge he looked out at the view and just thought what an amazing place it was, and he didn't want me messing up his idea of it by jumping from it. He also told me a bit about his past.

He'd actually had a really mixed up childhood. His dad kept leaving home and he was passed round the relatives like a dog no one wanted. He also went through drugs and stuff, but had finished with that long ago. He said that the reason he was telling me all this was to show how things changed. He said that the bad times he had been through had seemed inescapable at the time, but now they were just tiny distant memories. He said that when I was feeling bad I should imagine the problems like that – like I was looking back from ten years time and seeing how small it all was, or looking down from an aeroplane at a town and seeing how small it was compared to the big world.

I found that a pretty good thought. It was the first point of our conversation that I stopped thinking I was just putting up with this stuff until I could go back and finish the job.

After the coffee he made me go through all the people I knew that I might be able to trust to look after me for a couple of weeks. He said the best thing for me would be to get the hell away from town for a while, and recuperate, seeing how small things were from a distance.

The only person I could think of who seemed at all possible was my Uncle Jeff. He lived in Boston (all this happened way out in the sticks where I grew up). And he was about the only person in my family I hadn't offended lately. To start with I said I couldn't possibly go there, it would be too much of an imposition. But this guy (I never did find out his name) said that was stupid. I was just about to kill myself and I was worrying about social niceties? If this wasn't a crisis then what was?

So I let him persuade me, and that still wasn't enough. He insisted on driving me all the way there – 100 miles across country, and then on coming in to meet my uncle. He didn't tell my uncle what happened (though I ended up doing that myself to explain). He just came in to shake his hand and say that he was bringing me because I needed some help.

And then he just went. He didn't give me a number, and I didn't ask for one. So I don't know who he was. I was still in a funny mood, so I didn't realize what a huge thing he had done for me. My uncle thanked him, though of course he was a bit bewildered.

But he took me in. We called home next day to explain where I had got to. And I just stayed there for a month, not doing drugs, eating healthily and thinking. And then I realised this was a pretty nice town, so I looked around for work and a place to live. I ended up living around the block and working in a bookshop in town.

That guy saved my life by making me take a step back and think. And he was completely right. Now that I'm writing this ten years later, the problems that were getting to me then seem tiny, just like he said. I built a new life for myself, and then once I'd done that I managed to go home now and then and build a few bridges with the people I had upset. But from that time to this my real life has been here.

Supernatural
Experiences

A lot of this book is taken up with experiences that have entirely natural explanations. However there are a few accounts here that can only be described as supernatural.

Whether or not you believe in the supernatural, it is clear that for someone who does believe in it, a supernatural experience can be as powerful if not more so, in affecting the life of that person.

In the cases of Leila and Isla, as a rationalist one has to wonder if the messages they received from beyond the grave were in fact messages from their subconscious. But in the end it is immaterial whether or not these really are psychic visits or not. The effect that they had on these people is clearly real and that is the most important thing.

Leila, 23
Portland

My grandpa died when I was eight. I was very close to him – he had spent a lot of time looking after me when I was a kid, while my mother was at work. I knew that people died – my grandma had died when I was little. But it didn't really come home to me what that meant until he died.

I found him. I had stayed the night at his house, and when I got up in the morning the house was cold because he hadn't turned the heating on.

I went to his room to wake him up and he was just there, still in the bed, not breathing. He looked like he was asleep, but he wouldn't wake up.

I didn't know what to do. Luckily I knew how to use the telephone so I called my mother's house and told her that Grandpa wouldn't wake up. She came around as fast as she could and then she took me to stay with my aunt while she sorted things out.

They didn't let me go to the funeral, because they thought it would upset me, which seems pretty stupid as what could upset me more than seeing him dead? I was upset because I'd wanted to say goodbye to him. They meant well, but it was a shame I couldn't be there. Everyone kept telling me that Grandpa had gone to Heaven and trying to gloss over it. But finding him there had made me understand what it means to die.

Things were difficult for a while because my mother was too busy to look after me all the time. Instead of spending time with my grandpa, I got passed around

243

various friends and relatives during the week and then spent the weekend with my mother who was often too tired to do much playing, where Grandpa had always had time for me. I missed him terribly, but I had to grow up a bit and try to understand how difficult it was for my mother bringing me up on her own.

I had a very difficult, rebellious period in my teens and I think all of that fed into it. I was in trouble at school and did a lot of drugs with my friends. And strangely enough the thing that got me out of that period was a dream about Grandpa.

One day after I had been sent home from school, my mother was at the end of her tether with me, and we had a huge argument.

That night I dreamt about Grandpa. He was very angry with me. He shouted at me about how I was making life difficult for Anna (that's my mother), and told me I was being a spoilt brat. It was quite shocking, even though it was only a dream, because he hardly ever used to even raise his voice. He only shouted at me when I was being very foolish or doing something dangerous. So for him to shout it had to be a real problem.

I remembered the dream absolutely vividly when I woke up. I don't know if it was a kind of message from my grandpa's spirit. Or maybe perhaps there was a bit of me buried deep down that knew how angry he would have been at me for the way I was behaving. Either way it worked. I tried really hard to make things up with my mother. I stopped doing drugs and tried to get back on track at school.

Whatever the truth about that dream, I'm certain that

it was my grandpa's influence that turned my life around. Because either he spoke to my directly, or else it was a memory of the good influence he had on me that brought me back to my senses. He was a good man, and I've never had such a wise friend since then. I still miss him to this day, but at least now I like to think he would be proud of the way I live my life.

Isla, 29
Dundee

I went to a psychic a few years ago. I'd done a few similar things over time – palm readers, tarot cards and hypnotherapists. It was always interesting, but none of them really seemed that genuine in retrospect.

But this woman was extraordinary. She knew things about me that I had never told anyone. She knew that I had lost a child, and she knew what I was going to call it. I would swear that she was reading my mind.

She told me that there was a message from my mother (she died young). My mother said that I was "hiding inside myself." That's all – I was a bit bewildered by this and wanted to hear more, but she said she couldn't hear anything else. Just that she loved me and missed me. And of course I told her to tell her the same back – I was crying by this stage. It was spooky really. I absolutely believe that she really heard a message from my mother.

Then as I was about to leave, quite shaken by all the things she had said, she took my hand and told me to listen to what my mother had said. And she also said as a

245

parting shot, that I should find out what my husband was doing in the evenings. I almost slapped her I was so angry. We'd been married a couple of years and I trusted him completely.

I tried to ignore what she said. He often went for a drink with his friends in the evening or worked a bit late, and I tried not to think about what the psychic had been implying. But of course I couldn't forget it. I ended up following him one night, more to prove her wrong than anything, but of course he turned out to be going to some woman's house. I was devastated – I moved out immediately and went to stay with my sister. He kept coming round shouting at the windows to try and make me come home. He admitted what had happened but claimed it was a one-off, but I just didn't think I could trust him any more

I actually went back to the psychic to ask for advice. She wasn't much use. She didn't hear any more from my mother, and she told me that advice wasn't her thing. She even apologised for telling me about my husband, but said that she had felt it was somehow wrapped up with my mother trying to contact me, and that I needed to find out what was wrong in my life. She wouldn't charge me, and just told me that no one but me could decide what to do.

In the end I left town. I went and got a job right up here in Scotland, where I didn't know anyone, and started all over again. And it was the best thing I ever did. I realized what my mother had been trying to tell me. Back there in my hometown I had always been trying to live up to what other people expected of me – my father, friends, teachers and then my husband. It was only him letting me down like that gave me a total break from that. And then I started trying to work out what I wanted to do for myself, and realized it was quite different to how I had always lived my life there. I "came out of hiding" and became myself at last.

Tony, 40
Shropshire

In my twenties I lived in Paris. I didn't live particularly well. I drank and smoked too much, and I gambled in casinos. I earned enough money to get by, but I was starting to get into debt, because I was living an irresponsible lifestyle.

When what I am about to tell you happened I am ashamed that I was looking for a prostitute. I hadn't ever been to one, but it seemed like all the people I knew used them, and I was feeling frustrated. I had decided to venture out into Pigalle to the red light area and find a girl.

I was quite nervous as this was a first time experience for me. It was quite a misty night, which suited me well as I was nervous of being seen.

Then down a side alley, I almost walked into an old man. He came out of nowhere, and grabbed my arm. He said he had to talk to me. He told me that I was living a bad life, and that the only solution was to leave the city. He told me to live out in the country where there were less temptations and to build myself a new life. I didn't say a word. I was amazed that he seemed to know me (he knew my name for instance) and to know all about me. And he was giving me this quite solemn warning.

I asked him to come and talk to me in a café and he said that he had told me all I needed to know. I insisted so he indicated that I should lead the way. So I walked ahead, and after about three steps I looked back and he was gone.

I don't know if he was an angel, or my conscience or just a hallucination, but I took his advice anyway. I knew he was right, but I had been blasé about it. Now I got scared, and started to feel disgusted with the way I had been living.

I moved back to England and settled in a small village way out in the country. I married a local girl and raised a family here and have never regretted it for a single moment. I don't know how my life would have turned out if that hadn't happened to me, but I suspect it would have been much worse.

Carola, 32
Madrid

I first saw a ghost when I was ten. My parents took me to a house they were thinking of moving to. They took me to the room that would have been mine, and it seemed lovely.

But then I went up into the attic room. It was very cold up there, and there was a woman standing and crying. I didn't know what to do. I asked her if she was alright, but she just turned away and kept crying. I looked closer, and she was holding a knife, which had something dripping off it – it might have been blood, though it was hard to tell.

I was a bit scared, so I went to get my mother. She came straight back up with me, but there was no one there.

She was completely freaked out by it and immediately refused to buy the house. I didn't really understand, but she was saying to my father that she wouldn't share a house with a ghost.

She seemed to accept straight away that that was what I had seen – I found out later that she has seen a few ghosts in the past, so she was ready to believe me, where some parents might have thought I was playing a silly game.

It took me a while to realize that not everyone sees ghosts. You either can or you can't. I have seen them quite a few times in my life – they are often sad or disturbed, and it is something that I am very uncomfortable with, but that is an important part of my life whether I like it or not.

Leon, 28
France

I nearly died when I was in my teens. There was a fire in our house and I had to jump from the upstairs window to escape – I had breathed a lot of smoke, and had to get out because the heat was too intense. But I landed on hard ground and fell on hit my head.

I actually stopped breathing and had to be resuscitated. But the interesting thing was what I saw. I felt all the time completely wide awake and relaxed, even though everyone tells me I was unconscious – I knew what was happening, and I saw the road ahead. There was a strong white light in the air above me, and a path opened up – it is hard to describe exactly what I saw because it was not of this world.

Meanwhile I could hear all these people running around me, and I was vaguely aware of someone breathing into my mouth. But I was more interested in the path. There was a spirit there as well. She was smiling at me and holding out her hand. I held on to her for a moment and it was one of the happiest moments of my life.

After that I felt myself being dragged back into the world, and I woke up in terrible pain. I had broken my ankle, and cracked a couple of ribs in the fall, and my head was bleeding where I had hit it.

While I had been seeing the door I had felt none of this, but now I was back on the wet ground with smoke everywhere and fireman still fighting the blaze.

I was in hospital for a couple of weeks recovering. At night I was visited by the spirit I had met. I call her she, but I am not really sure what gender she is. She tells me things about the past, and sometimes she brings other spirits to meet me or to talk to me. They are not all as gentle and pleasant as her. I am lucky because she is my spirit guide and she is very good.

I hear things that the dead want to tell me. I suppose I could work as a psychic or something, but the messages are not always coherent or wise to pass on. It is quite an upsetting talent at times. I do believe that having been so near to passing on to the other side opened up a channel in me, and now I am able to communicate with spirits. This has some quite strange consequences in my life. But mostly I find it reassuring. Because I know that when I do eventually die, my spirit guide will be waiting for me once again, but this time we be able to got through that door and along the path to wherever you go to next.

Small Steps,
Everyday Roads

Sometimes it is the smaller things in life that matter. A change of lifestyle or a new friend, giving up a bad habit or changing your appearance. These things may seem minor from a distance, but in your own life these matters can be of great importance.

All of the stories in this section relate to the relatively simple, domestic details of life. Decisions about a change in everyday behaviour, and the basic but tremendously difficult decisions people make to overcome addictions such as alcohol and cigarettes. These are matters that can take on a great importance in people's lives.

I think it is important to remember that, if you want to change your life, it is often these supposedly minor aspects of life which are the best starting place. The very act of exerting control over your everyday environment and behaviour can give you the confidence you need to achieve great things.

Wanda, 38
Wyoming

I gave up smoking last October. I had tried so many times to give up, because I felt it was slowly ruining my health – I was a heavy smoker, and I had started to feel short of breath all the time. Then there's the smell of cigarettes on you all the time, the coughing in the morning. Really it's a horrible habit, but it is so hard to give up.

I'd tried various strategies – nicotine gum, using books about how to do it, giving up at the same time as friends. They all gave up but I kept being a recidivist. I was a serial relapser.

Finally my friends suggested a hypnotherapist. He had helped her make a diet work, and the results had been very effective.

I went to see him a few times. Basically we talked about all the things I liked about smoking and the triggers that made me want to have a cigarette. Then we talked about all the nasty things about smoking – the health, the ash, the smell and so on.

He hypnotized me two or three times only. I don't exactly know what he did, but for some reason it completely worked. Basically I would still have the urge to have a cigarette at particular times, but at the same time I would remember all the bad things – instead of remembering these things later and feeling guilty.

Somehow he kind of reprogrammed my mind – I already had all these thoughts there, but they would be there at different times – he made them come at the same time, and that means that I managed to overcome the urges.

It might not work for every one, but it sure did for me. I felt much better once I managed to quit. I felt fitter and healthier, and I even felt more confident because I didn't have this sensation of going round in a haze of smoke any more. I think it's fair to say it really did change my life.

Carey, 28
Leeds

I had a very interesting experience when I was at college. I had always, always had long hair, ever since I was child. I have nice hair and I used to be proud of it, maybe a bit too proud.

I didn't really connect with people at college. I felt that they were treating me like I was a bit of a bimbo, some kind of Barbie figure. I am quite attractive, at least I am told that I am. A lot of girls used to treat me in a funny way, very competitive or hostile.

In fact this had probably been happening to me all through my late teens, but it wasn't the same at school. I had friends who had always known me, and who treated me the same when we all became teenagers. But away at college it was very noticeable.

My first term was a bit miserable, largely because of this and the fact that I didn't really make friends.

After Christmas at home, I went back to college in January, and I had a real new broom kind of feeling, what with New Year's resolutions and everything. And what I decided to do was to cut my hair off.

I had a really short pageboy kind of hair cut – the

furthest extreme I could go to. When I looked in the mirror I was shocked at how different I looked. It was like a completely different person.

There were two effects. Firstly I felt like I was starting again – people reacted to me as though they had never met me, in fact a few of them did a complete double take as they worked out that it was really the same person they had met last term.

More importantly it did make a significant difference to how people treated me. Instead of treating me as pretty but dim, they saw me as someone more androgynous, and as a result they listened to me when I spoke.

Now there's a degree to which that means that people are shallow – the fact that they could behave so differently simply because of my appearance. I was aware of that aspect of the change, and it has affected the way I view my appearance since then.

But really at that age, my main concern was just to get on with people and make friends. And by having a fresh start I managed to do that. I started to see the way I had dressed and looked a bit girly and childish and felt that I had managed to move on a step in life.

Since then I've had long hair and short hair in all sorts of styles. I've never been as fragile so I'm better equipped to ignore what people think of me. I'm more confident in myself. But at that age something as simple as a change of appearance really made a big difference.

Tibor, 32
Prague

I wasn't a particularly happy child. I was an only child, and I didn't get on very well at school. I felt I was not too clever and that I didn't have lots of good friends around me.

My parents were nice people, but they were very straightforward and respectable. They wanted me to learn to be a useful member of society so they encouraged me to read and write and do maths and play sports. But they weren't at all interested in artistic things – I believe they saw art as bourgeois and not very respectable.

I always wanted to draw, but all I had to draw with was plain pencils and it was not very satisfying. It's hard to believe, but we had absolutely nothing in the house with which I could paint or draw properly. And at school we focused on very functional utilitarian subjects – art was a tiny part of the curriculum and not one that we were encouraged to spend too much time on.

One time when I was about seven, my uncle came to visit. He saw me drawing and helped me. It seemed that he was very good indeed at drawing – I remember being amazed by a drawing he did of my mother sitting reading.

We didn't see my uncle very often at all, but a few weeks later he came round again and he had bought me a present. It was a big pack of colored pencils and pad of nice paper.

I was of course delighted with this. My parents weren't that impressed, but didn't do anything to discourage me. I wasn't very good to start with of course, but my uncle had spotted that I had an eye for shape and that I was interested in getting things down in pictures. All I needed was the tools.

I was much happier after that because I had a hobby that absorbed me completely. I could spend days working on one tiny drawing – I learned to work in miniature because I always had problems getting enough paper.

Drawing stayed with me through my whole life – I learned to paint later when it got easier to get the materials, but drawing was always my preferred form. I eventually became a designer, and my drawing is an important part of what I do even today.

When I feel down I can still cheer myself up by remembering the sheer joy I felt when I first opened that beautiful package of pencils – every color you could imagine and more. It seemed like my whole life had been in black and white and then suddenly I had color!

Carly, 24
Glasgow

I used to be determined to have an operation to enhance my breasts. They were quite small, and as a teenager I was very self-conscious about them. I felt that boys only paid attention to girls with larger ones. And also everywhere I looked on the television or in the magazines there were famous girls who had done exactly that, or who had in other ways used plastic surgery to become more successful. It seemed like the obvious thing to do.

From the age of eighteen I worked hard to save up the money. It took me two years of overtime and working in a bar at the weekends and I was finally getting closer to being able to pay for it.

During this time I did go out with a few boys. I do think I suffered from low self-esteem though, and they weren't always nice to me. That only fed back into my conviction that the operation was what I needed.

Finally, the summer after my twentieth birthday I had all the money, and I went for a consultation. At the end of it the surgeon booked me on for the operation a few weeks later.

That night I went out with friends and met a lovely man called Iain. We immediately hit it off and started to see each other every day. After about a week I plucked up the courage to tell him I was going to be having the operation. I actually thought he would be pleased – because he already liked me, but now I would have better breasts too!

But in fact he was horrified. He hated the whole idea of doing something like that to your body. And he thought that the sorts of girls who did that were bimbos, worrying more about their appearance than about what's inside. At first we argued about it. I felt he wasn't being supportive, or that I could persuade him round to my viewpoint.

We almost split up over it, it was such a bad argument. In fact at the end of the night I stormed out, determined to have nothing more to do with him and to go ahead with the operation. But when I woke up the next day I came to my senses – I was terrified of losing the nicest man I'd ever met, so I went round and we kept talking about it.

Eventually I agreed to at least postpone the operation and think about it. And we stayed together.

Over time we talked more and more about it, and I started to realize he was right. He was also smart because he didn't just say I was stupid about the whole thing. He told me what a good job I had done in saving up so much money, and pointed out how if I put that kind of determination to work in other ways I could do really well for myself.

I had been a kind of bubble where I only paid attention to information that reinforced what I wanted to do. But actually it is quite a strange thing to do. Besides which, he liked me as I was. Being loved by such a nice man did wonders for my self-esteem! And gradually it started to seem like a strange thing for me to have wanted to do in the first place.

I'm really grateful to him now. I read so many horror stories about operations that go wrong or have to be reversed later. But also I feel that if I'd had the operation my self-esteem would have been completely false. It would have been based on something about me that wasn't real. So in a way it would have been like hating myself and only liking me for being a person I wasn't, I you see what I mean.

I'm still together with Iain. I spent some of the money I'd saved up on my half of a lovely holiday in Antigua last year. And the rest of it is staying in the bank towards the deposit on the house we're hoping to buy together.

Calum, 29
Belfast

I've just enrolled for a college course, studying English and History. That may not sound that big a deal, but I left school at fifteen and I came from a background where everyone looked down on students.

I always worked as a labourer or builder, and I thought that would be my life. Getting drunk at weekends and getting into fights, then working hard through the week. But my brief time at school wasn't completely wasted. I am reasonably literate and numerate, and I enjoy reading books. But I mostly stuck to bestseller kinds of things, true crime and so on.

The main thing that changed my mind was a girl I went out with about five years ago. I used to tease her about the strange books she read, but when she explained them to me I started getting interested, and I ended up reading all sorts of different things.

I also started reading more history. I was always interested in the Second World War because my grandfather fought in it. But I started to read more about not just the actual wars, but about the causes and the build up to it. And I kept finding that I wanted to take that further back to understand how the first world war ended, and then how it started, and then how the empires who fought it had come about, and so on.

I just got more and more of a curiosity about all these things that you could learn from books, and the internet helped too, because once that arrived I found a wealth of information. The more I know the more I see that the internet is unreliable as a source, but it still has loads of information to get you interested.

But all this was something I could do at home, as a private hobby. On the outside I was still the same laddish guy I had always been, and I certainly didn't talk to my mates about some of the stuff I read. In the end I thought that this was all wrong. I was actually a different person to the way I was living my life. So I spent a year working hard and saving, and doing an evening course that I needed to qualify for the college.

And now here I am, a student at the old age of twenty-nine. It's a bit weird because a lot of the others are ten years younger than me. But on the other hand I know about all sorts of things (like life . . .) that they don't yet, so it's not all bad.

It took a bit of courage for me to do this because it's such a break from the way my life was going. Some of my friends are proud and supportive, others think I've gone soft and can't understand it. But I don't care. I just think this is something I have to do. I know it will change my life, I'm just not exactly sure how yet.

Ray, 33
Detroit

I have given up drinking. At Christmas I got drunk way too often, and at least once it was a serious session with Jack Daniels and Tequila and everything I could grab. I was sick for two days.

But even before that I had started to think I was drinking too much. I had got to that stage where there weren't that many days where I didn't drink at least a bit.

And my idea of "a bit" had crept up over time. Once that would have meant a bottle of beer. Now it meant a four pack and a few shots. It was starting to make me feel heavy and unfit, because every morning I felt a bit rough, and I never quite felt up to exercising.

In January I decided to quit for a while, as a New Year resolution. I've done that before and it never lasted. But this time I also joined a gym at the same time. I started to go in the mornings before work, and then again after work. It's only down the road and it's open late, so I also got in the habit of occasionally popping in later, at about nine or ten o'clock. It's quite a sociable place, and I often chat to a few people while I'm working out. I'm not doing any kind of extreme bodybuilding, just general exercise.

Since I've been going to the gym, I've found I don't want to drink in the same way. It's like the moments in the day when I used to want a drink – after work and later on, I can just go and work out instead. And if you drink you don't enjoy the next day's workouts. And because I also talk to people at the gym, I don't miss the atmosphere of the bars I used to go to.

You could almost say I haven't given up the drinking through my own willpower – I've just found a new habit to replace it with. Because going to the gym becomes as much of a little addiction in its own way. But it's a much healthier habit, and one that makes me feel much better about myself.

Love and Friendship

I was delighted to receive so many accounts that stressed the crucial importance of the basic bonds of love and friendship.

Each of the people whose writing I have included in this section goes out of their way to stress the role that love has played in their life. Here we see examples of the love between husband and wife, parent and child, and the lifelong importance that can be taken by a friend who is not a part of our family.

I was especially intrigued by Anya's account of "falling in love" with her child. It is easy to forget that the bond between parent and child is not a given. Not all parents bond with their children, and not even all mothers find it easy to love their offspring. In Anya's case, she started out without this bond, but then discovered it in herself later on.

Love is not something we should ever take for granted in our lives, not even the love that our parents feel for us. When you love someone you also make a commitment to that person. Without the support we receive from those we love and who love us, life would be a great deal more difficult.

Hans, 45
Amsterdam

Everything changed for me the day I met my wife. Of course she wasn't my wife then – just a girl called Anna that I met at a friend's party. I had never really been serious about any girl before. But as soon as I met Anna I knew I had met someone I wanted to spend my life with.

People ask me how I could be so sure. It's hard to explain if it hasn't happened to you. It's partly that she was so beautiful of course. But it was also the way we spoke to each other, the things we had in common, the jokes we both laughed at. We ended up leaving the party (it was a weekend lunch) and going for a long walk through the city together. All the way I was desperately hoping she felt the same about me as I did about her. All the shops we wanted to look at, all the things we noticed about other people seemed to match up. But also there were things she knew I didn't – I respected her and wanted to know more about her but I knew that we had to be together somehow.

At the end of the afternoon I asked her out the following weekend. She wasn't free because she was going away on holiday so I had to wait two weeks to see her. It was terrible because I was terrified that it would turn out to have been my imagination, or that she wouldn't show up. But as soon as I saw her again I knew it was all exactly the same. There hasn't been a day since then when we didn't

271

at least speak, and I love her just as much as I ever did, even now twenty years later.

I changed then because for the first time I really cared about someone other than myself. I loved my family and friends of course, but it's different. For her I would have done absolutely anything. I wanted to look after her and protect her. It's more like the feeling you have when you have your first child. Of course she doesn't really need looking after. If anything it is her that looks after me! But somehow we get along and look after each other. I'm very lucky to have her in my life.

Den, 28
Copenhagen

When I came to college here, I had a miserable time. I was a really country boy, and I had no idea about all the trendy things that people liked to talk about. I was good with computers, but that just made me a nerd to the people I talked to.

For the first couple of months it was really hard going. Then one day I was in the food hall at the college, and a boy called Pet sat next to me. He asked me if I was alone and I made a joke about it, something a bit gloomy.

We talked while we ate. Then afterwards he walked through to the bar and came back with a glass of vodka. He said "Drink that. We're going out."

I'd been out with a few people and not enjoyed it, but I had a brilliant time with Pet. He was much more urban than me, but in a funny way he was also a bit of a loner. It's partly because he is extremely clever. He finds people boring, and can't be bothered, but that comes across as being very elitist or sardonic. But as it happens he found me amusing, partly because I have quite a black sense of humour.

We got very drunk and staggered back. He fell asleep on my sofa. From then on we were the best of friends, and it completely transformed my life. I got to know a few more people steadily. But rather than feeling that I was excluded from the crowd I started to see that a lot of the people in the crowd were a bit foolish and that they were being conformist out of fear of being seen to stand out.

Pet was very good at seeing that, partly because he has such a low opinion of people. Actually sometimes he takes it too far. There are people who aren't brilliant or bizarre who are worth talking to. Over time we have both mellowed a bit, and he is not as hardline as he once was.

But at that time it was very important to find that, while I wasn't a part of the mainstream, I could find a few friends who enjoyed standing outside the mainstream laughing at it.

When we left college we set up a business together, starting from a digital magazine, and then expanding into all types of communications and media. We have done very well as partners. We shout at each other sometimes, it would be hard not to. But from the first day he put that glass of vodka in front of me, he has been a major part of my life, and someone I look up to as a friend.

Anya, 29
Switzerland

I had terrible post-natal depression after the birth of my first child Natasha. I basically rejected her for the first two months. I felt terrible and empty and I blamed her. I didn't love her at all, and I hadn't when she was inside me, and now she had been born I felt as if my life was over.

Luckily my husband and family managed to cope with that very dark time in my life. I had medication for the depression, which did help a bit. But still I was very down. I know it is partly a physical reaction but the emotional effects of that are devastating.

For all that time I barely held the child. My mother spent a lot of time looking after her – I would hardly even look at her I was so messed up.

Then one day, I remember it very clearly, my mother had to leave me in the house with the baby. She was worried about whether or not I could cope – she spent ages talking me through what I had to do, and how to feed and change her. I had done these things a few times but only sporadically and unenthusiastically.

Eventually the door shut and there I was alone with the baby. I was quite scared actually. After an hour or so she woke up from her nap and started to cry.

I went in and asked what she was crying about. She looked up at me with those big eyes that babies have, and tried to reach out towards me. I didn't really know what I was doing, but I picked her up and started to rock her. She just made that little chirruping noise they make and settled down. If I stopped rocking she grumbled, but mostly she just lay there staring up at me.

It was something about the way she looked at me. So trusting in spite of all the ways I had let her down. I started crying and crying. She just kept staring at me. I couldn't put her down, so the tears were just running down my face and making my blouse wet.

Eventually she started complaining again and I realized she was hungry so I put her in her basket and went to sort myself out. I got my face cleaned up and managed to follow my mother's instructions on preparing milk (she was on formula because I had refused point blank to breast feed).

What happened that day was I fell in love with my child. For some women this happens the first time they see them. Others develop an attachment while they are still inside growing. But I hadn't and it had taken me until now for it to happen. I always was a late starter.

But once it happens, that's it, you are in love. From then on I wanted to be with her and to watch her all the time. I still needed help. The depression didn't magically go away overnight. But now I had something counterbalancing it, in my love for Natasha. And when things seemed too dark, all I had to do was to go and watch her and I felt a tiny spark of hope or happiness again.

I especially liked to watch her when she was asleep. They are so trusting and so completely helpless, and when they are asleep they are beautiful. It's not easy looking after a child, but the one thing that makes it worthwhile is the love you feel for them.

Kenneth, 38
Spain

My life changed for the better the day I met my wife Jenna.
She is completely different from me. She's so beautiful
and clever and outgoing, and I am quite a quiet person.
When I met her I thought she was wonderful, but I never
thought she would be interested in me.

We were working together in a temporary job, where
we all used to go to the bar or the café at the end of the
day, so I used to talk to her a lot, but I thought nothing of
it. But then one day she asked if I wanted to go for a beer
after work.

I thought she just wanted someone to talk to or
something, but she made it clear that she was interested in
me. I couldn't believe I was so lucky.

I spent the first few years we were together fearing
that it might not last, but we became more and more
in love the longer we were together. She changed me
in many ways. She brought me out of myself and
encouraged to do things I might otherwise have been
too self-conscious or worried to do. Before I was with
her I would never have gone waterskiing and I would
never have been brave enough to leave my job to set
up a business when I had an idea for one.

But she encouraged me and told me that you have to
take your chances, and that she was prepared to work
twice as hard to make it happen for me.

The new business was a big success quite quickly, and
then when we needed to expand she came to work with
me, so now we run the business together.

I am grateful to her for so much that I can't explain it

all in a few pages. She looked after me after my parents died, and helped me through the death of a close friend. We have two children who I adore, and she is such a good mother to them.

If she hadn't come along I sincerely think that my life would have been very different. I might have found myself in other ways and developed on my own, but with her I have had a truly happy and fulfilled time. We have done some crazy things together and some memorable things together, and I will always love her no matter what happens.

Sandy, 29
Florida

I met my best friend Annie when we were both at pre-natal classes. I was eighteen and a single mother (or about to be . . .). It was pretty stupid of me to get pregnant really. My mother wanted me to consider an abortion or adoption or something, because she thought I was just a kid and I wouldn't be able to cope. I wasn't at all sure I would be able to, but I couldn't lose my child no matter what went wrong.

So there I was, quite isolated, losing touch with all my school friends and not getting on too well with my family. I was so lucky to meet Annie. She's three years older than me, and has a fine husband, so she's in a pretty different situation to me.

I liked her right away because she wasn't taking it all too seriously. Some of the people there were acting like they were at a funeral or something. We started going out to have cake and milkshakes and chatting about everything.

She took me under her wing from the start. She treats me like I'm her little sister or something. She told me once that she wished she had brothers and sisters but she doesn't. But she's better than a sister to me – more like a best friend, sister and aunt all rolled into one.

When the babies were born we were round each other's houses all the time. Neither of us really knew what to do (it was her first one too) but we figured that we'd likely do a better job if we worked it out together.

So while her husband would be at work, we'd be in her kitchen gossiping and trying to work out how to keep a baby happy. I really had to get back to work as fast as I could, so Annie used to look after my little boy Roy a couple of afternoons a week. I couldn't make a lot of money, but I needed something to survive. She used to cook me an awful lot of meals too, which helped. She'd never admit she did it because she felt sorry for me, but I know that she could see I needed a bit of support in my life at that stage.

My mother did help me a bit, but we'd always had a funny relationship, and she's always acted disappointed that I ended up a single mother, while Annie always just took me at face value.

Later on, Annie encouraged me to start writing. Her husband worked at the local paper, and he was able to pay me to do a few short pieces. I started reviewing local cafes and shops where you could go with a baby. It made a huge difference in my life. And they really went out on a limb to get me the work. I left school early and even though I'm not stupid, I had a lot of catching up to do to even be able to do a professional job.

But after a year or so things started looking much better. I found other bits and pieces of freelance writing and other work, which meant I could work late at night at home, and make enough money to give my boy a decent way of life. Of course no sooner than I got my life sorted out, I was stupid enough to have another baby (that's it though, no more for me!), a little girl I called Maisy, and yet again Annie was there to help me and bail me out. She's got three kids now, and my two and hers play together all the time. They're like one big extended family really.

I don't tell Annie all the time how much I appreciate what she did for me. She's my friend and she didn't just do it out of pity – we really like each other and have the best times together. But when I do stop to think I praise the Lord that I met her when I did. She's a truly wonderful friend and I am so lucky to have her in my life.

Mina, 56
Arizona

My current husband is my second husband. I had quite an unhappy marriage which lasted five years in my early twenties, and it really knocked me back. My first husband used to treat me quite badly. He cheated on me and lied to me, and even hit me a few times, and I lost all self-confidence for a while, even after I got my act together to leave him.

I lost myself in work and in my thirties, while I dated quite a lot, I always steered well away from anything that looked like commitment. I felt like I had been there, done that, and it had turned out as badly as it could. I really didn't want to get hurt again.

Then not long after I turned forty I started going out with Jack. I had just about settled for growing old with my cats and being a mad old lady dressed in purple, but then he came along. He treated me like a princess from the start. He was so charming and thoughtful and we got on like the best of friends. It went a long way beyond anything I had known since I was young. I found myself falling in love once again.

But it still took me a long time to come round to realizing that things had changed. He asked me to marry him after we'd been together about six months and I just laughed it off. I really wasn't going to do it again.

I think he was a little bit hurt when I did that, but he didn't let it get to him. He kept on being the same old Jack, and after a while in spite of my misgivings I moved in with him. It felt absolutely normal. I was happier than I had been for years.

He asked me to marry him on Midsummer's Eve. He did it in a very romantic way. He took me on a drive up our favourite hill and then surprised me by pulling out a ring and getting down on his knee (not for long though – it was pretty dusty down there!)

And though I'd vowed not to, I said "yes" and started crying. It was a wonderful moment in my life and I've never regretted it.

I still find him incredibly attractive, and I still want to hug him whenever I see him. I thought that might go away as I got older but it hasn't in the slightest. He hasn't changed much since I met him. He's got a bit grayer but he is still the most charming, polite and helpful man you could imagine.

I realize now that I was just unlucky with the first one. He really put me off marriage and that was a shame as I spent a large part of my life shying away from real relationships. But in the end Jack saved me and I've ended up with such a happy marriage. I try to thank him for that as often as I can, and now I'm telling you because I want everyone to know how much I love him.

Never Say Die

One thing I noticed while I was compiling this book was that the whole idea I had started from, of one day that changes your life, isn't quite adequate enough to describe many life-changing experiences. Because a lot of the ways that people change their lives come about because of their persistence and devotion to an ideal or aim.

When someone works over time to change their life and finally enjoys the fruits of their persistence, it may be that there is a single day that epitomizes the struggles they have had.

For instance Tom spent months learning to recuperate after an accident. At the end of it he was able to walk unaided. But that isn't really the day when his life changed. In fact it changed in little steps and increments over a long period, with all his hard work and effort, until the day came when he could look back and say, "I did that – I really changed my life."

The same is true of Angela who spent so long scrimping and saving in order to get herself into a position of financial freedom. It was her assiduous work and concentration on a goal, an everyday determination that led to the day when she could finally do one simple thing that changed her life for the better.

Thankfully we won't all face the specific challenges that were faced by some of the writers in this section. However I do think that we could all learn something from the attitude these people adopted about their problems.

Each faced up to a problem and identified a path of action that would help to mitigate it. And each then had the courage and drive to carry out a plan, and never gave up because of adversity.

How many small resolutions, targets and goals do we all have in our own lives? In small ways, if we can try to apply this kind of determination to our own lives, we may be able to change them more than we realize.

Tom, 41
Texas

I had a terrible car accident eight years ago. I was lucky not to die. They had to cut me out of the car. My legs were so badly damaged they had to amputate both beneath the knee.

I was terribly depressed afterwards. I felt like I had thrown my life away in a moment of stupidity – the crash was completely my fault – I was alone in the car, with no cars near, and I went off the road on a corner because I was going too fast. I ended up tangled up with a couple of trees and a metal fence, and as a result the car was crushed around me.

I had all kinds of weird dreams about my feet, and even when I was awake I would keep sensing that I could feel them, only to look down and see the bandages.

They made me prosthetic feet which attached to the remaining part of my legs. Learning to walk again was the hardest thing I have done in my life. To start with it really hurt me even to try to stand for a moment. The stumps would swell and give me pain, and I would have to give up, and just lie there crying with frustration at how my life had been wrecked.

They had a wonderful physiotherapist who worked with me over weeks and months in the hospital. My family were coming in to see me as often as they could, but they were never there when I was doing the exercises.

After a couple of weeks I came out of the hospital in a wheelchair. I had to stay at my mother's, as I couldn't cope on my own. The stairs in my house would have defeated me if nothing else did.

I got pretty good at coping without walking, though it was very frustrating. I hated being dependent on my mother.

Meanwhile I was going to the hospital on a regular basis, and trying to walk using the rails they have there. The physiotherapist gave me exercises to build up the muscles I was going to need. You basically have to learn to walk in a very different way because the balance is different, and you really strain the new muscles you have to use for the first few weeks.

Finally I got better and better. I started to be able to walk short distances at the hospital. I told my mother I would be walking home soon, and she said that once I could we would have a party. I wasn't sure I wanted that as it put a lot of pressure on me, but I agreed.

We agreed to do it the following Saturday. My brother drove me to the hospital and we left the wheelchair behind, as I was going to be coping without it. I was fitted with my feet – the first time my brother had seen them so he was completely fascinated and kept asking all kinds of silly questions about them which made me and the physiotherapist laugh. I had bought her some flowers to thank her for all her work.

Then he helped me out to the car. I was walking, but he opened doors and so on. The walking felt pretty good by now. It could still be tiring, but I had built up the basic strength in the important muscles.

Back at my house, people had started to arrive for the party, and my family and a few of my closest friends came out onto the lawn to see me come in. I got out of the car and stood and walked up the drive by myself, and they all applauded me. It was a bit silly, but it was also very touching. I had worked so hard to get out of the depression and to learn how to do this, but mostly people had been nervous to talk about it. I think they worried I might be in a wheelchair forever and didn't want to raise false hopes in me.

I don't mind saying I cried a few times at that party. I saw a lot of good people, and perhaps for the first time I really appreciated the goodwill that I was getting from them. Everyone had really pulled together for me, and even if they couldn't help directly, they had been sending me positive thoughts and feelings. And now that I could walk again, I at least felt that I had overcome one fundamental problem, but only with the help of all these people.

Obviously I couldn't spend the whole party standing or walking, but I did as much as I could to show people how I was doing. At the end of the day I was exhausted but very happy with how the party had gone. At the very end I gathered my family together in the kitchen to tell them how grateful I was to them. I realized that I had been so wrapped up in my problems that I had never really done that, but now finally I had the perfect opportunity to show them my gratitude.

Angela, 33
Lancashire

I spent three years working incredibly hard to pay off my mortgage. I split up with my boyfriend when I was twenty-seven. We owned a flat together and I had to take on a pretty big mortgage to buy him out of his half. I was determined to hang on to it because it was my security in life.

289

We had been planning on going travelling, and letting out the flat. But once we split up that idea was no longer practical. I was really angry because he had messed everything up. It was his fault, because he was the one who was unfaithful, but I won't bore you with all the details.

So now I could rent out the flat, but the rent would barely cover the mortgage, and I needed money to live off if I was going to travel.

What I decided to do was to work really hard to pay off the mortgage. It was quite crazy really. I drew up a budget and cut out everything I could. I lived off very simple home cooked food – a lot of baked beans, vegetable pasta and eggs.

I gave up smoking and cut drinking right down. I didn't have any little treats like lunchtime sandwiches and so on. I cycled to work and got rid of the car, and that saved a lot straight away. I cut up my credit cards and didn't spend a penny on clothes unless I absolutely had to.

But on top of that I had to earn more money. I took a job as a waitress in a local restaurant. I had waited when I was younger, but it was really hard work to go back to. I would work all day in the office and then go out and work in the evening, then fall into bed exhausted. The restaurant was a very friendly one with a bar where people just come in for a drink at the weekend, so I had kind of a social life, but it was mostly based around the bar.

I also did quite well from that job as the pay was supplemented by tips, which could be pretty generous at times.

I was quite maniacal in my determination looking back. I didn't have a holiday in those three years, because I couldn't bear any setbacks in my plan. If I even bought a chocolate muffin I would feel guilty all day (it was pretty good for my health and weight as well . . .).

I think there is also a degree to which I was feeling very damaged by the breakdown in my relationship. I had expected to grow old with him, and suddenly it was all gone. A lot of our friends were mutual friends that I didn't want to see all the time, so turning my life on its head and disappearing into my shell in this way was partly a negative reaction to that as well as a positive drive. I don't know which was most important, but the main thing is that I was extremely motivated.

After two years of this I was getting a bit bored, and also I was behind schedule, so I took on even more work. I advertised in local newspapers for basic computer lessons – I used them all the time at work so I'm pretty competent. I ended up teaching four or five local people to use their new computers, doing basic word processing, the internet and email and all that kind of stuff. That was the last little bit of money I needed.

Just before the end of the third year I finally had enough money to settle the mortgage. I remember the day with great pleasure. I took the day off work made an appointment at the bank, and wrote out a cheque for the full remaining amount. Then I went to the nearest bar and bought a small glass of champagne to celebrate.

It was a marvellous feeling. I had felt really trapped by my situation, as though I had a huge burden dragging me back. Now I had managed to free myself from that burden, and I felt light as air as a result.

It was only a few weeks to Christmas so I didn't want to let the restaurant down. I ended up working there through to New Year's Eve, which became a mixture of New Year Party and farewell party for me.

I had quit work and arranged for a tenant to move in by the end of January and I was ready to go. It was quite extraordinary being able to spend little bits of money again. After so long of being mean and penny-pinching, even spending a few pounds on a magazine seemed like a wicked decadence. But it felt wonderful as well, because I had achieved exactly what I set out to do.

I spent the best part of a year travelling and saw some amazing places. When I moved back, I was in a very different state of mind, and the fact that I now owned my home put me in a very different situation with regard to money. I was able to live a much more relaxed life. I met my new boyfriend in the last few weeks of travelling, and after a few months he moved in with me. He pays rent though. I didn't do all that work only to support him! Actually he insists, because he sees it as the only fair way to deal with the situation.

I'm so glad I went through what I went through. But I really wouldn't ever want to do it again.

Kelvin, 28
Hull, UK

It took me the best part of eight years to qualify as a solicitor. I'm a single father. I had twins with my girlfriend when we were both at college (it was an accident). She couldn't cope and she left me with them. We see her occasionally now, but she has a different life, and it all seems like a long time ago.

So I had to get through college supporting my kids. I worked part time at all sorts of things, and my family helped whenever they could. The twins are marvellous, but they are hard work, and I used to have days when I would spend the day at college, the four hours from five to nine at telemarketing firm I worked at and then come home to relieve my sister from looking after the twins, at which point I'd have to give them their bath, get them to bed, do the washing and ironing, eat some food, and then fall asleep exhausted only to do it all again the next day.

I hadn't always meant to be a solicitor, but about four years ago I decided that rather than leave college and struggle to find work, I would live with it a bit longer and try to get a professional qualification. So I stayed on, and did a conversion course.

But it was hellishly difficult. I had to defer the course halfway through the first year because of a financial crisis that meant I needed to take more paid work on and I was getting behind with my studies.

Still I went back, because I was determined to see it through. The last year and a half I was just hanging on in there, because the end was in sight.

Then, finally, I qualified. That was the big day for me. I had a job lined up, and I went from struggling to having a little more financial room for manoeuver overnight. Not that it is ever easy. I am still the one in charge, and I have to spend a lot of time outside of work with my children so that I don't feel that I am missing out.

But I can afford babysitters now and then, and for proper childcare after school. I can even go out on a date now and then, so who knows, maybe I will even fall in love again some time, although it is hard because my family always has to come first. I can never thank my family enough for helping me get to this point. But I'm a little bit proud of myself as well because it has been a long road, and I have stayed on it.

Niamh, 46
Cork, Ireland

I lost seven stone in a year of dieting. I had become very unhappy about the way I had put on weight.

I had dieted before but only in a sporadic way, and the weight always crept back. What was different this time is that I set myself a very specific target. It was my parents' anniversary later that year, and I had some a black dress that used to fit me, that I was now still too big for. I decided to try and get down to a weight where I could wear that dress to their party.

I was very rigorous in my dieting. I cut a lot of foods out completely. I had an absolute minimum of carbohydrates and had a lot of meals that were basically salad or vegetables and fruit.

I also went to the gym twice a day. I had always put off doing this because I didn't want to be there in my leotard feeling fat in front of a group of strangers. But I made the decision that I needed the gym to make me keep to a real exercise routine – a bit of aerobics in front of the television had never worked for me, and now I needed some serious training.

I paid a personal trainer for the first few sessions and we developed a range of routines that would stretch me enough to really burn some energy.

And that was it really. No gimmicks, no magic ingredients. Just sheer hard work and focus. To start with I didn't feel like it was working, as the weight went very slowly in the first two months. I'm not sure why, but I tend to think my body had to adapt to a different regime or maybe I had to work to speed up my metabolism before the effects really kicked in.

Either way, the third to sixth months were very effective, and a lot of weight went. I started to fell really good.

Then it got a bit harder again. It was winter and I found it harder to do without comfort food. And the pounds seemed to go really slowly. Sometimes I would even slip back slightly.

But the main thing is I never completely lost heart and I never gave up. Even when I felt like I wasn't getting anywhere, I kept grinding away, and gradually I managed to shed a few pounds more and then a few more.

By the week of the party I was back down to nearly the weight I had been when the dress fitted. I tried it on, and it still felt very slightly tight, so I bought another dress just in case. But I kept dieting and exercising right up to the day of the party, and finally that morning I tried the dress on and it fitted perfectly.

I felt absolutely brilliant and my family were wonderful too. They all rallied round and made me feel like I had really achieved something amazing. My parents had a lovely party, and for once I relaxed and enjoyed myself a little.

Since then I haven't put the weight back on at all. I enjoy being this size again so much, I have remained vigilant. I don't have to diet all the time, but I still go to the gym. I have a few days each week where I am very cautious, then the rest of the time I just have to be mildly careful about what I eat, and the weight stays about the same. I am more alert, more active and happier. In fact I feel like a completely different person.

Happy Stories

I very much wanted to finish this book with some cheerful stories. Along the way we have heard from people in all kinds of situations – some happy, some confused and some tragic.

But life is full of happiness as well as sorrow and confusion, and it is good to be reminded of that periodically.

I found these stories inspiring, each in their own way. In particular I was impressed by the attitudes shown in the last two stories. Alison has clearly been through some difficulties in her life. But she has also made some extraordinary discoveries. Firstly her ability to see herself as lucky in all situations is a great talent. But beyond that, the idea that her happiness is greater because it was so hard won is something I found to be an inspiration. It holds out the hope that even someone who is going through a difficult time can take heart from the idea that any happiness they find their way through to will be all the sweeter because of the obstacles they have overcome.

And finally Daniel expresses an idea that I agree with completely – that the best way to live your life is as though the world is a miracle, and as though every day might be the day your life changed.

Carol, 39
Washington State

I used to be quite poor. I was on my own, with three kids, after my husband left home. I never heard from him again or got any support for the kids, and I worked part time to get by.

My neighbour (I'll call her Elsa – you'll see why later I don't tell you her real name) was a bit richer than me. Her husband hadn't left home, and he had a reasonable job. They weren't wealthy or anything though, just a normal family. We spent a lot of time doing things together as our kids were similar ages. We used to take turns looking after them after school so that we had a bit of time to get things done.

On 3 July 1999, (I always remember the day because it was the day before the Fourth) Elsa came round to my house in the day. She seemed very agitated. She had flushed cheeks and quite wild looking eyes.

I wondered what was the matter, but actually it was good news. Amazing news. She had won the lottery.

It was a big win – over six million dollars. I hugged her and told her how pleased I was for her – I knew it would make all the difference to her life.

But then came the really extraordinary bit. She wanted to give half of it to me! She had been thinking and thinking about it and she wanted me to have the same chance she was getting.

I asked her whether her family and other friends would mind, but she said that her family were all fine and she would be able to get them presents and stuff. And her other friends she could get treats for. But she felt that I

301

had had such a hard time over the years that I deserved this more than anyone she could think of.

I even argued with her, saying she should just give me a gift if she wanted. But the thing is she wanted to be able to explain to other people that it was a joint ticket, that it was a syndicate between us, so that no one asked her why she had given me so much. We had actually done this years earlier, and then I had stopped doing it as part of an economy drive, so that was what had given her the idea.

I ended up asking her to think this over and come back the next day, but she refused. She'd actually already told her husband that story, and she told me I couldn't make her back down because it would get her into trouble.

Eventually I ended up agreeing. It was such a wonderful thing for her to do for me, and she assured me over and over that her share was more than enough for anything she could imagine.

I've never told anyone about this. Everyone knows about the lottery win, but only Elsa and me know that it was really her ticket. I see her as almost an angel in my life because the kind thing she did transformed my life. Money isn't everything, but it does make a big everyday difference. Even after I gave a lot of money to charity I still ended up with a completely different life to the one I had had before.

I still see Elsa all the time. We both bought better houses with some of the money so we aren't neighbours anymore, but we are still the best friends possible, and she knows I am still as grateful as anyone could be for the beautiful thing she did.

Connie, 75
Edinburgh

My life changed the day I married my husband. We've been married for fifty-two years and I still love him as much as ever.

I can still see the wedding day as though it was yesterday. His hair was jet black and slicked back with cream, like the boys did in those days. He looked like Denis Compton if you remember who he was, or maybe a bit like Clark Gable in *It Happened One Night*.

He had hired a beautiful morning suit and I was wearing my mother's wedding dress, a marvellous white lacy dress with the full white veil and my grandmother's pearls.

Our families didn't always get on, but that day was a special day for everyone. We didn't spend a lot of money, but it still really meant something. We were married in the church and the reception was in the church hall. But we had a band because Donald's brother knew some boys who had a band and they came to play for free as a favour. It was a great party, we were up to all hours dancing and I dare say, having a few drinks.

The presents we got were all the things we needed for a house, because of course we hadn't moved in together. That night was the first night I went back with him to our new little house. It was all different in those days.

We went to the South Coast, to Bournemouth for the honeymoon, because we had relatives down there. Everything about the wedding and honeymoon went so well.

We didn't have much in those days. It was not long

303

after the war, and there were not many treats and possessions around. But I can't help thinking that the things we had meant more to us then. I can still remember every detail of the clothes I took on honeymoon, and of the lovely presents that people gave us. And we certainly knew how to have a party back then, despite what people think now.

It was the happiest day of my life and if I ever need cheering up these days I think back to it, and remember how wonderful I felt.

Alison, 38
Canada

I had a very difficult childhood. I don't want to tell you about that though. You just need to know that at the age of twenty I was quite an anxious, depressed person, and a lot of that was a result of my background.

But I survived all the things that had been difficult, and things were staring to level out. But still I wasn't really happy.

What changed things for me occurred one day when I was in Dublin. I had gone there to visit a friend and one day I was out walking. There was this old guy lying on the ground. He was obviously a drunk, and probably homeless too. I thought he might be hurt, so I offered him a hand and helped him to sit up on to a bench.

He said thanks and then he gave this funny crooked smile and said "See, I'm the luckiest man in the world." I laughed and asked why, and he said, "Because even after everything that I've been through, I'm lying here, a disgrace to everyone, and someone like you comes and give me hand. How could I not be lucky."

I just smiled and gave him some cigarettes that he asked for and said goodbye. But what he said stuck in my mind. The fact that someone who seemed to be in miserable circumstances could see himself as the luckiest person in the world, really stayed with me.

When I got back to Canada, I went on thinking about this, and on one rainy Sunday I got my notebook out and made a list of everything that was good and bad about my life. There were plenty of bad things. But quite a few of the things that were bad had already improved a bit, or were in the past. There were, however, more good things than bad, and more of the good things were in the present or the future.

I wrote at the top of the page "Why I'm the luckiest woman in the world," and put it into my purse. There was something genuinely cathartic about doing this. I think it crystallised some thing that had been slowly changing in my life anyway, without my truly understanding them. Slowly I had dealt with many bad things, and had learned how to turn from bad things to good things.

But until then I had always felt like the fact that this was such an effort proved that I was bogged down in the past and would never escape. Now I realized that life is hard work, but that the hard work does lead you towards better places.

Since then I think I have been happy more than I have been sad, which is the opposite of how I was before. Anytime bad things happen to me, I just say to myself that I am the luckiest woman alive. And even when this is just an ironic way of making the bad things less bad, I remember the humour of that old man in Dublin and if nothing else that cheers me up.

But I really do think I'm lucky because I appreciate the good things about my life. I wonder if you can really be happy unless you have been sad at some time in your life. If everything was always easy, then you wouldn't have to struggle for happiness. But the fact that I had to work so hard to find happiness makes me savour it all the more now that I have it.

Daniel, 28
Pennsylvania

You asked about the day my life changed. I don't have one single day in mind. Lots of things have happened to me in my life, both good and bad, but I'm not sure I could pick one day out over any of the others. Meeting my partner, my parents splitting up, passing my exams, my first girlfriend, and our first break-up, my first job, the first time I lost a job, my grandmother dying . . . All those things were important to me in different ways, and there have been plenty of other things that I could mention.

I always try to remember something that Albert Einstein said, which I read when I was young. He said something like, "There are two ways to see the world. Either you can expect nothing to be a miracle, or you can expect everything to be a miracle." And he was suggesting that the latter was the best approach to life.

I think it's a great thing for him to say. Here you have one of the great intellects of mankind, whose scientific work is all about demonstrating an explanation for everything, about reducing mystery and conquering the cosmos. But his attitude is that mystery and awe are crucial. This world is an amazing place, and no matter how well we understand or categorize it, we should never forget how amazing it is that we exist at all.

So one of my rules in life is to try and remember that quote, and to see the world as a miraculous place. The other rule I have always had relates more directly to your question. I have been through enough turmoil, and enough extraordinary changes in the world to know that you never know what is going to happen in life. You think you have everything worked out and then everything gets tipped on its head.

The map of the world gets rewritten, or there is some big terrorist attack. You think you're never going to meet a girl, then you walk round the corner and there she is. You think your job is going great then the company gets bought out. Things come out of the blue all the time, and you have to be prepared for that.

And the worst thing you can do is resist. You can fight against things you disagree with, but once your world changes you can't waste time wishing that you had the old world back or trying to act as though nothing has happened. You have to adapt and cope and look for the new problems and solutions in your life.

So I try to live every day as though it might be the day my life changes. I try to fully appreciate the things I have, because any day they might be taken away. I try to live in the moment and plan for the future, but when things do change I don't want to be stuck in the past.

I think that if every day I treat my life this way it gives

me a more intense understanding of the ways in which I am lucky and blessed by life, but it also allows me to let go and move on when I have to.

Afterword

I found this book fascinating to compile. When I started I had no idea what kinds of responses I would get to a simple question – to tell me about the day your life changed. In the end I was overwhelmed by the accounts I received.

Many of the stories I was told were deeply personal. It is always humbling and intriguing to see how varied people's experiences are in life. A lot of the accounts in this book are concerned with difficult events in people's lives. But I hope that the final message is one of optimism.

The concepts of pessimism and optimism only exist because of the fact that people's lives are deeply unpredictable. We have to evolve strategies to deal with the complexities of life.

Optimism is not necessarily going to lead one to a luckier life, but a positive attitude often helps us to overcome the rockier periods in life without feeling victimized. Of course some would argue that a certain pessimism or at least stoicism can be valuable in protecting oneself from disappointment. However I tend to think that a pessimistic outlook can prevent us from seeing the best things in life as they develop, and indeed from taking the chances that life offers.

Some of the accounts in this book describe people who had an inspiration or insight, but who then developed a plan of action and carried it through until they succeeded in transforming their lives. This is an

311

easier thing to achieve if you remain positive in the face of temporary setbacks and adversity.

The main message I ended up taking from the accounts in this book was that even in the face of terrible events, people are capable of showing fortitude, grace and courage. Anything can happen and some of the things that will happen to us in the future will be difficult.

If we can take the good luck and bad luck with equal equanimity, and if we can show integrity and bravery in our dealings with the world, then we have the best chance possible of surviving the slings and arrows of fortune.

The last thing I should do is to warmly thank anyone who shared their experiences with me. I have gained a great deal from the experience, and I hope that in reading this book you have shared some of the pleasure and fascination I had in making it.